Heirloom Doilies™

A Collection of Favorite Crochet Patterns

HOUSE of
WHITE
BIRCHES

PUBLISHERS
SINCE 1947

Heirloom Doilies

Editor: Laura Scott
Copy Editor: Cathy Reef
Editorial Assistant: Marla Freeman
Pattern Editor: Agnes Russell
Assistant to Editorial Director: Jeanne Stauffer
Editorial Director: Vivian Rothe

Photography: Nora Elsesser, Tammy Christian, Sandy Bauman
Photography Assistant: Linda Quinlan

Production Manager: Vicki Macy
Creative Coordinator: Shaun Venish
Production Artist: Scott Ashley
Production Coordinator: Sandra Ridgway Beres
Production Assistants: Patricia Elwell, Cheryl Lynch, Matthew Martin

Publishers: Carl H. Muselman, Arthur K. Muselman
Chief Executive Officer: John Robinson
Marketing Director: Scott Moss

Printed in the United States of America
First Printing: 1995
Library of Congress Number: 95-78058
ISBN: 1-882138-11-2

Every effort has been made to ensure the accuracy and completeness of the instructions in this book. However, we cannot be responsible for human error or for the results when using materials other than those specified in the instructions, or for variations in individual work.

Special thanks to the following for photography on location: Limberlost State Historical Site, Geneva, Ind., Page 106; Schug House Inn, Berne, Ind., Page 114; Swiss Village Retirement Community, Berne, Ind., Pages 34, 100 and 124.

Cover: *Kaleidoscope Centerpiece,* pattern begins on Page 115.

Do you remember the sounds, smells and sights of your grandmother's home? Most of us had the pleasure of spending time with our grandmothers during our childhood years — and what impressionable years are they! Everything in Grandma's house always seemed so clean, crisp, and well, old — from the large, heavy antique furniture to her delicate china dishes adorned with pretty flowers. In the evenings, Grandma would sit in a rocking chair or on the sofa and relax with her crocheting. As a child, watching Grandma crochet seemed like magic. How could she turn simple white thread into something so beautiful, delicate and intricate as a doily? Yet she did, and then carefully pressed and starched her doily so every stitch could be clearly admired. Then she would carefully select a place in her home to display her newest creation.

Today, most of our grandmothers are gone and many of their precious belongings have been scattered into the homes of our families. I hope each of you has at least one of your grandmother's crocheted doilies for yourself. If not, one can always be grateful for the love of crocheting that she has passed on to you.

Capture the memories of those warm days spent with your grandmother with this beautiful collection of heirloom doilies. Many of these doilies will remind you of the ones she once crocheted with such loving care. As you crochet each doily, you'll find yourself relaxing into the soothing rhythm of crochet as you work round upon round. You'll also find yourself reminiscing about those fond days of youth. If you are fortunate, perhaps you'll have a young child or grandchild by your side watching your work progress with wide eyes and awe.

From your grandmother to you, and from you to your grandchildren, crochet is a treasured craft that reaches across and connects the generations. May these doilies become a part of your family tradition.

Laura Scott
Editor, Heirloom Doilies

Table o

Contents

Floral Beauties

*Nature's delicate work of art, flowers are a cherished source
of beauty, fragrance and inspiration for people of all walks of life. Each
of the five floral doilies in this chapter captures the precious beauty of
flowers and will grace your home all year long. So select your favorite colors
of crochet thread and begin stitching roses, pansies, dahlias, poinsettias
and more floral delights!*

Pansy Garden

Dahlia Delight

Rose & Pineapple Treasure

Flower Dance

Perfect Poinsettias

Pansy Garden

Like velvety pansies that cheer the heart every warm summer day,
so this enchanting doily will delight you every month of the year.

Getting Started

Experience Level
Beginner

Size
Doily center: 8"
Diameter overall including flowers: 12½"

Materials
- Crochet cotton size 10 (150 yds per ball):
  1 ball each white and shaded purple
- Size 7 steel crochet hook

Gauge
3 sts = ¼"; 3 shell rnds = 1"

Pattern Note

Join rnds with a sl st unless otherwise stated.

Pansies
Make 16

Rnd 1: With shaded purple, ch 6, join to form a ring, ch 7 (counts as 1 dc, ch 4), [2 dc, ch 4] 4 times in ring, 1 dc in ring, join in 3rd ch of beg ch-7.

Rnd 2: Working in ch-4 sps, [sc, dc, 6 tr, dc, sc] in each of next 2 ch-4 sps (2 small petals completed), [sc, dc, 8 tr, dc, sc] in each of next 3 ch-4 sps (3 large petals completed), join, fasten off.

Doily

Rnd 1: With white, ch 6, join to form a ring, ch 3 (counts as first dc), work 15 dc in ring, join. (16 dc)

Note: When working following dc rnds, work dc sts between dc sts, not in the top of sts.

Rnd 2: Ch 3 (counts as first dc), dc in same st as beg ch-3, work 2 dc in each rem dc around, join. (32 dc)

Rnd 3: Ch 3, dc in each dc around, join. (32 dc)

Rnd 4: Rep Rnd 2. (64 dc)

Rnd 5: Ch 3, dc again in same sp, ch 1, sk 2 dc, 2 dc in next sp between dc, ch 1, [sk 2 dc, 2 dc in next sp between dc, ch 1] rep around, join in 3rd ch of beg ch-3.

Rnd 6: Ch 3, dc, ch 2, 2 dc in same ch-1 sp as joining, sk 4 dc, [2 dc, ch 2, 2 dc in next ch-1 sp, sk 4 dc] rep around, join. (16 shells)

Rnd 7: Sl st into ch-2 sp of shell, ch 3, dc, ch 2, 2 dc in same ch sp, ch 1, [shell of 2 dc, ch 2, 2 dc in next ch-2 sp of shell, ch 1] rep around, join.

Rnds 8–13: Sl st into ch-2 sp of shell, ch 3, dc, ch 2, 2 dc (beg shell), shell of 2 dc, ch 2, 2 dc in each shell around, adding 1 more ch between shells on each rnd, join. *Note: On Rnd 8 ch 2 between each shell, on Rnd 9 ch 3 between each shell, continue in this man-*

Continued on Page 13

Dahlia Delight

Twenty luscious motifs reminiscent of giant dahlias form the border of this magnificent centerpiece doily.

Getting Started

Experience Level
Intermediate

Size
20" in diameter

Materials
- Crochet cotton size 30 (500 yds per ball): 2 balls white
- Size 9 steel crochet hook

Gauge
3 shell rnds = ¾"; 7 dc = ½"

Pattern Note
Join rnds with a sl st unless otherwise stated.

Pattern Stitches
3-tr cluster (3-tr cl): Retaining last lp of each tr on hook, tr in next 3 sts, yo, draw through all lps on hook.

4-tr cluster (4-tr cl): Retaining last lp of each tr on hook, tr in next 4 sts, yo, draw through all lps on hook.

Inner Motifs

First Motif
Make 7

Rnd 1: Ch 12, join to form a ring, ch 1, 24 sc in ring, join. (24 sc)

Rnd 2: Ch 5 (counts as first dc, ch 2), sk 1 sc, [dc in next sc, ch 2, sk 1 sc] rep around, join in 3rd ch of beg ch-5. (12 ch-2 sps)

Rnd 3: Ch 3 (counts as first dc), 3 dc in ch-2 sp, [dc in next dc, 3 dc in ch-2 sp] rep around, join in 3rd ch of beg ch-3. (48 dc)

Rnd 4: Sl st in next dc, ch 3, dc in each of next 2 dc, ch 3, sk 1 dc, [dc in each of next 3 dc, ch 3, sk 1 dc] rep around, join in 3rd ch of beg ch-3. (36 dc)

Rnd 5: Ch 4, retaining last lp of each tr on hook, tr in each of next 2 dc, yo, draw through all lps on hook (beg cl), ch 5, sl st in top of cl (picot), ch 4, sc in next ch-3 sp, ch 4, [3-tr cl over next 3 dc, ch 5, sl st in top of cl, ch 4, sc in next ch-3 sp, ch 4] rep around, join in top of beg cl, fasten off.

Second Motif
Rnds 1–4: Rep Rnds 1–4 of First Motif.

Rnd 5: Work beg cl, ch 2, sc in picot of First Motif, ch 2, sl st in top of beg cl, ch 4, sc in ch-3 sp, ch 4, 3-tr cl over next 3 dc, ch 2, sc in next picot of First Motif, ch 2, sl st in top of cl, ch 4, sc in next ch-3 sp, ch 4, [3-tr cl over next 3 dc, ch 5, sl st in top of cl, ch 4, sc in next ch-3 sp, ch 4] rep around, join in top of beg cl, fasten off.

Third Motif
Rnds 1–4: Rep Rnds 1–4 of First Motif.

Rnd 5: Work beg cl, ch 2, sc in 4th picot of

Second Motif, ch 2, sl st in beg cl, ch 4, sc in ch-3 sp, ch 4, 3-tr cl over next 3 dc, ch 2, sc in 3rd picot of Second Motif, ch 2, sl st in top of cl, attach next 2 picots to First Motif, continue remainder of motif in usual manner, fasten off.

Fourth–Seventh Motifs

Continue to work motifs in same manner, attaching working motif to previous motif and then to First Motif. Join Seventh Motif to previous, First and then Second to join. There will be 1 motif at center and 6 motifs around the outer edge.

Doily

Rnd 1: Attach thread in 2nd free picot of any motif, *[ch 9, sc in next picot] 3 times, ch 9, dtr in last picot, dtr in first picot of next motif, ch 9, sc in next picot, rep from * around, join.

Rnd 2: Ch 3 (counts as first dc), [11 dc in each ch-9 sp, dc in each sc, sk first dtr, dc in next dtr] rep around, join in 3rd ch of beg ch-3. (360 dc)

Rnd 3: Ch 5 (counts as first dc, ch 2), sk 2 dc, [dc in next dc, ch 2, sk 2 dc] rep around, join in 3rd ch of beg ch-5. (120 ch-2 sps)

Rnd 4: Ch 3 (counts as first dc), 2 dc in ch-2 sp, dc in next dc, ch 6, sk 2 ch-2 sps, [dc in next dc, 2 dc in ch-2 sp, dc in next dc, ch 6, sk 2 ch-2 sps] rep around, join in 3rd ch of beg ch-3. (40 groups of 4 dc)

Rnd 5: Ch 3 (counts as first dc), dc in each of next 3 dc, ch 3, sc in ch-6 sp, ch 3, [dc in each of next 4 dc, ch 3, sc in ch-6 sp, ch 3] rep around, join in 3rd ch of beg ch-3.

Rnd 6: Ch 4, retaining last lp of each tr on hook, tr in each of next 3 sts, yo, draw through all lps on hook (beg cl), ch 5, sl st in top of cl (picot), ch 5, sc in ch-3 sp, ch 3, sc in next ch-3 sp, ch 5, [4-tr cl over next 4 dc, ch 5, sl st in top of cl, ch 5, sc in next ch-3 sp, ch 3, sc in

next ch-3 sp, ch 5] rep around, join in top of beg cl.

Rnd 7: Sl st into picot, ch 1, sc in same picot as beg ch-1, ch 10, [sc in next picot, ch 10] rep around, join in beg sc.

Rnd 8: Ch 3 (counts as first dc), 13 dc over ch-10 sp, [dc in next sc, 13 dc over ch-10 sp] rep around, join in 3rd ch of beg ch-3. (560 dc)

Rnd 9: Ch 4 (counts as first dc, ch 1), sk 1 dc, [dc in next dc, ch 1, sk 1 dc] rep around, join in 3rd ch of beg ch-4. (280 ch-1 sps)

Rnd 10: Sl st into ch-1 sp, ch 3 (counts as first dc), 1 dc, ch 2 and 2 dc in same ch-1 sp (beg shell), ch 7, sk 4 ch-1 sps, [shell of 2 dc, ch 2 and 2 dc in next ch-1 sp, ch 7, sk 4 ch-1 sps] rep around, join in 3rd ch of beg ch-3. (56 shells)

Rnd 11: Sl st into ch-2 sp of shell, work beg shell, ch 4, [shell in next ch-2 sp of shell, ch 4] rep around, join in 3rd ch of beg ch-3.

Rnd 12: Sl st into ch-2 sp of shell, work beg shell, ch 4, insert hook under ch-7 of Rnd 10 and ch-4 of Rnd 11, complete a sc around both chains, ch 4, [shell in next shell, ch 4, insert hook under ch-7 of Rnd 10 and ch-4 of Rnd 11, complete a sc around both chains, ch 4] rep around, join in 3rd ch of beg ch-3.

Rnd 13: Sl st into ch-2 sp of shell, ch 1, sc in same ch sp, ch 8, [sc in next ch-2 sp of shell, ch 8] rep around, join in beg sc.

Rnd 14: Ch 3 (counts as first dc), 9 dc over ch-8 sp, [dc in next sc, 9 dc over ch-8 sp] rep around, join in 3rd ch of beg ch-3. (560 dc)

Rnds 15–18: Rep Rnds 9–12.

Rnd 19: Sl st into ch-2 sp of shell, ch 1, sc in same ch-2 sp as beg ch-1, ch 10, [sc in next ch-2 sp of shell, ch 10] rep around, join in beg sc.

Rnd 20: Ch 3 (counts as first dc), 14 dc in ch-10 sp, [dc in next sc, 14 dc in next ch-

10 sp] rep around, join in 3rd ch of beg ch-3.

Rnd 21: Ch 5 (counts as first dc, ch 2), sk 2 dc, [dc in next dc, ch 2, sk 2 dc] rep around, join in 3rd ch of beg ch-5, fasten off.

Outer Motifs
Make 20

Rnds 1–4: Rep Rnds 1–4 of First Inner Motif for all 20 Outer Motifs.

Rnd 5 (First Motif joining): Work beg cl, ch 5, sc in any ch-2 sp of Rnd 21 of Doily, ch 5, sl st in top of cl, [ch 4, sc in ch-3 sp, ch 4, work 3-tr cl, ch 2, sk 3 ch-2 sps of Rnd 21, sc in next ch-2 sp, ch 2, sl st in top of cl] twice, ch 4, sc in ch-3 sp, ch 4, work 3-tr cl, ch 5, sk 3 ch-2 sps of Rnd 21, sc in next ch-2 sp, ch 5, sl st in top of cl, [ch 4, sc in ch-3 sp, ch 4, work 3-tr cl, ch 5, sl st in top of cl (picot), ch 4, sc in ch-3 sp] 8 times, ch 4, join in beg cl, fasten off.

Rnd 5 (Second Motif joining): Work beg cl, working to the left of previous motif, ch 2, sl st in 2nd free picot, ch 2, sl st in top of cl of working motif, ch 4, sc in ch-3 sp, ch 4, 3-tr cl, ch 2, sl st in next picot of joined motif, ch 2, sl st in top of working motif cl, ch 4, sc in ch-3 sp, ch 4, 3-tr cl, ch 5, sk 1 ch-2 sp of Rnd 21, sc in next ch-2 sp, ch 5, sl st in top of cl, [ch 4, sc in ch-3 sp, ch 4, 3-tr cl, ch 2, sk 3 ch-2 sps, sc in next ch-2 sp, ch 2, sl st in top of cl] twice, ch 4, sc in next ch-3 sp, ch 4, 3-tr cl, ch 5, sk 3 ch-2 sps of Rnd 21, sc in next ch-2 sp, ch 5, sl st in top of cl, [ch 4, sc in ch-3 sp, ch 4, 3-tr cl, ch 5, sl st in top of cl, ch 4, sc in ch-3 sp] 6 times, ch 4, sl st to join in beg cl, fasten off.

Continue to rep Second Motif joining to within last motif.

Join last motif to previous motif, to Doily, and then to First Motif.

—Designed by Dorothy Newman

Pansy Garden

Continued from Page 9

ner, ending with Rnd 13 which will have ch 7 between each shell. At end of Rnd 13, do not fasten off, sl st into next ch-2 sp of shell.

Attaching Pansies

Note: *When attaching pansies to doily, the middle large petal is attached to shell and each large petal at each side is attached to large side petal of pansy to each side. Small 2 petals are on outer edge of doily.*

Rnd 14: Pick up pansy, sc from shell into center st of center large petal, [sc in each st to the center of next large petal of pansy, pick up another pansy, sc into side petal center to join pansies, sc in each st toward center st of center large petal, sc in next st at center, sc in ch-2 sp of shell] rep around, joining pansies to doily.

Once all large petals are attached to doily, continue to sc around outer edge of doily, attaching the rem half of large petal and 2 small petals together. Fasten off.

—Designed by Alma Perry

Rose & Pineapple Treasure

Two all-time favorite motifs, the pineapple and the rose, are featured in this beautiful, timeless doily.

Getting Started

Experience Level
Advanced

Size
14" in diameter
Large Rose: 1⅞" in diameter
Small Rose: 1½" in diameter

Materials
- Size 10 crochet cotton (350 yds per ball): 1 ball white
- Size 5 steel crochet hook

Gauge
1 shell = ½"

Pattern Notes
Always sc between picots in 2-picot lp and to right of picot on 1-picot lp.

Join rnds with a sl st unless otherwise stated.

Pattern Stitches
Shell: [3 dc, ch 2, 3 dc] in st or sp.

1-picot lp: Ch 2, picot, ch 2.

2-picot lp: Ch 1, picot, ch 2, picot, ch 1.

Small Rose
Make 3

Rnd 1: Ch 4, join to form a ring, ch 5, [dc in ring, ch 2] 5 times, join in 3rd ch of beg ch-5. (6 ch-2 sps)

Rnd 2: Sl st in sp, [sc, hdc, 3 dc, hdc, sc] in each ch-2 sp around, join in first sc. (6 petals)

Rnd 3: [Ch 4, sl st from back to front in first sc in next petal] 6 times, end with last sl st in beg sl st. (6 ch-4 sps)

Rnd 4: Sl st in ch-4 sp, [sc, hdc, 5 dc, hdc, sc] in each ch-4 sp around, join in first sc, fasten off.

Large Rose
Make 1

Rnds 1–4: Rep Rnds 1–4 of Small Rose, do not fasten off.

Rnd 5: [Ch 6, sl st from back to front in first sc of next petal] 6 times, end with last sl st in beg sl st. (6 ch-6 sps)

Rnd 6: Sl st in ch-6 sp, [sc, hdc, 7 dc, hdc, sc] in each ch-6 sp around, join in first sc, do not fasten off.

Doily

Rnd 1: Sl st to first dc of petal on Large Rose, ch 1, sc in same dc, *[ch 5, sk next 2 dc, sc in next dc] twice, ch 5, sc in first dc of next petal, rep from * around, ending last rep ch 2, dc in first sc. (18 ch-5 lps)

Rnd 2: Ch 1, sc in same place, *ch 6, sc in next ch-5 lp, rep from * around, ending last rep ch 3, dc in first sc.

Rnd 3: Ch 1, sc in same place, *ch 7, sc in next ch-6 lp, rep from * around, ending last rep ch 3, dc in first sc.

Rnd 4: Ch 1, sc in same place, *ch 7, sc in next ch-7 lp, rep from * around, ending last rep sl st in first sc.

Rnd 5: Sl st in lp, [3 sc, picot, 3 sc, picot, 3 sc] in each ch-7 lp around, join in first sc, fasten off.

Rnd 6: Attach thread in center sc between 2 picots, ch 3, [2 dc, ch 2, 3 dc] in same sc (beg shell), *[2-picot lp, sk next 2 picots, shell in next center sc between picots] twice, [2-picot lp, sk next 2 picots, sc in center sc between picots] 3 times, 2-picot lp, sk next 2 picots, shell in center sc between picots, rep from * around, ending last rep 2-picot lp, join in 3rd ch of beg ch-3.

Rnd 7: Sl st to ch-2 shell sp, ch 3, [2 dc, ch 2, 3 dc] in same sp, *[1-picot lp, sc between picots of 2-picot lp, 1-picot lp, shell in next shell sp] twice, [1-picot lp, sc between picots of 2-picot lp] 4 times, 1-picot lp, shell in next shell sp, rep from * around, ending last rep 1-picot lp, join in 3rd ch of beg ch-3.

Rnd 8: Sl st to ch-2 shell sp, ch 3, [2 dc, ch 2, 3 dc] in same sp, *[ch 3, sc in 1-picot lp, 2-picot lp, sc in next 1-picot lp, ch 3, shell in next shell sp] twice, 1-picot lp, sk next lp, [sc in next lp, 1-picot lp] 3 times, shell in next shell sp, rep from * around, ending last rep 1-picot lp, join in 3rd ch of beg ch-3.

Rnd 9: Sl st to ch-2 shell sp, ch 3, [2 dc, ch 2, 3 dc] in same sp, *ch 3, sc in ch-3 lp, [1-picot lp, sc in next lp] twice, ch 3, shell in next shell sp, rep from * once, ch 3, sc in next lp, [1-picot lp, sc in next lp] 3 times, ch 3, shell in next shell sp, rep from first * around, ending last rep ch 3, join in 3rd ch of beg ch-3.

Rnd 10: Sl st to ch-2 shell sp, ch 3, [2 dc, ch 2, 3 dc] in same sp, *ch 3, sc in ch-3 lp, [1-picot lp, sc in next lp] 3 times, ch 3, shell in next shell sp, rep from * once, [1-picot lp, sc in next lp] 3 times, 1-picot lp, shell in next shell sp, rep from first * around, ending last rep 1-picot lp, join in 3rd ch of beg ch-3.

Rnd 11: Sl st to ch-2 shell sp, ch 3, [2 dc, ch 2, 3 dc] in same sp, *ch 3, sc in ch-3 lp, [1-picot lp, sc in next lp] 4 times, ch 3, shell in next shell sp *, ch 2, 3 dc in same shell sp, rep from * to * once, ch 3, sc in next lp, [1-picot lp, sc in next lp] 3 times, ch 3, shell in next shell sp, rep from first * around, ending last rep ch 3, join in 3rd ch of beg ch-3.

Rnd 12: Sl st to ch-2 shell sp, ch 3, [2 dc, ch 2, 3 dc] in same sp, *ch 3, sc in ch-3 lp, sc in next lp, [1-picot lp, sc in next lp] 3 times, ch 3, shell in next ch-2 sp *, ch 1, shell in next ch-2 sp, rep from * to * once, 1-picot lp, sk next ch-3 lp, [sc in next lp, 1-picot lp] 3 times, shell in next shell sp, rep from first * around, ending last rep 1-picot lp, join in 3rd ch of beg ch-3.

Rnd 13: Sl st to ch-2 shell sp, ch 3, [2 dc, ch 2, 3 dc] in same sp, *ch 3, sc in ch-3 lp, sc in next lp, [1-picot lp, sc in next lp] twice, ch 3, shell in next shell sp *, 2-picot lp, shell in next shell sp, rep from * to * once, ch 3, [sc in next lp, 1-picot lp] 3 times, sc in next lp, ch 3, shell in next shell sp, rep from first * around, ending last rep ch 3, join in 3rd ch of beg ch-3.

Rnd 14: Sl st to ch-2 shell sp, ch 3, [2 dc, ch 2, 3 dc] in same sp, *ch 3, sc in ch-3 lp, sc in next lp, 1-picot lp, sc in next lp, ch 3, shell in next shell sp *, 1-picot lp, sc in 2-picot lp, 1-picot lp, shell in next shell sp *, rep from * to * once, [1-picot lp, sc in next lp] 5 times, 1-picot lp, shell in next shell sp, rep from first * around, ending last rep 1-picot lp, join in 3rd ch of beg ch-3.

Rnd 15: Sl st to ch-2 shell sp, ch 3, [2 dc, ch 2, 3 dc] in same sp, *ch 5, sc in ch-3 lp, sc in next lp, ch 5, shell in next shell sp *, ch 3, sc in next lp, 1-picot lp, sc in next lp, ch 3, shell in next shell sp, rep from * to * once, ch 3, sc in next lp, [1-picot lp, sc in next lp] 5 times, ch 3, shell in next shell sp, rep from first * around, ending last rep ch 3, join in 3rd ch of beg ch-3.

Rnd 16: Sl st to ch-2 shell sp, ch 3, [2 dc, ch 2, 3 dc] in same sp, *ch 5, sc in next sc, ch 5, shell in next shell sp *, ch 3, sc in ch-3 lp, [1-picot lp, sc in next lp] twice, ch 3, shell in next shell sp, rep from * to * once, ch 3, sc in next lp, [1-picot lp, sc in next lp] 6 times, ch 3, shell in next shell sp, rep from first * around, ending last rep ch 3, join in 3rd ch of beg ch-3.

Rnd 17: Sl st to ch-2 shell sp, ch 3, [2 dc, ch 2, 3 dc] in same sp, *ch 3, sc in next sc, ch 3, shell in next shell sp *, ch 3, sc in ch-3 lp, [1-picot lp, sc in next lp] 3 times, ch 3, shell in next shell sp, rep from * to * once, ch 3, sc in next lp, [1-picot lp, sc in next lp] 7 times, ch 3, shell in next shell sp, rep from first * around, ending last rep ch 3, join in 3rd ch of beg ch-3.

Rnd 18: Sl st to ch-2 shell sp, ch 3, [2 dc, ch 2, 3 dc] in same sp, *ch 3, sc in next sc, ch 3, shell in next shell sp *, ch 3, sc in ch-3 lp, [1-picot lp, sc in next lp] 4 times, ch 3, shell in next shell sp, rep from * to * once, ch 3, sc in next lp, [1-picot lp, sc in next lp] 3 times, ch 3, pick up Small Rose, sl st from back to front in first dc of any petal, sl st along edge in [hdc, 2 sc, hdc, dc] of rose, ch 2, sc in next sc between 1-picot lps, ch 2, sk 2 dc of rose, sl st in next 2 dc and hdc of rose, ch 3, sc in 1-picot lp, ch 3, sl st in next hdc and 2 dc of rose, ch 2, sc in next sc between 1-picot lps, ch 2, sk next 2 dc of rose, sl st in next dc of rose, sl st along edge

in next [hdc, 2 sc, hdc, 2 dc] of rose, ch 4, sc in next 1-picot lp, [1-picot lp, sc in next lp] 3 times, ch 3, shell in next shell sp, rep from first * around, ending last rep ch 3, join in 3rd ch of beg ch-3.

Rnd 19: Sl st to ch-2 shell sp, ch 3, [2 dc, ch 2, 3 dc] in same sp, *ch 1, shell in next shell sp, ch 3, sc in ch-3 lp, [1-picot lp, sc in next lp] 5 times, ch 3, shell in next shell sp, ch 1, shell in next shell sp, ch 3, sc in next ch-3 lp, [1-picot lp, sc in next lp] 3 times, 1-picot lp, sk next 2 dc of rose going upward, sc in next dc of rose, 1-picot lp, [sc in first dc of next petal, 1-picot lp, sk next 3 dc of rose, sc in next dc, 1-picot lp] twice, sc in 2nd dc of next petal, [1-picot lp, sc in next lp] 4 times, ch 3, shell in next shell sp, rep from * around, ending last rep ch 3, join in 3rd ch of beg ch-3.

Rnd 20: Sl st to ch-2 shell sp, ch 3, [2 dc, ch 2, 3 dc] in same sp, *sc in next ch-2 shell sp, [1-picot lp, sc in next lp] 7 times, ch 3, shell in next shell sp, sc in next ch-2 shell sp, [1-picot lp, sc in next lp] 4 times, 1-picot lp, sk next lp, sc in next lp, [1-picot lp, sc in next lp] 4 times, 1-picot lp, sk next lp, sc in next lp, [1-picot lp, sc in next lp] 3 times, ch 3, shell in next shell sp, rep from * around, ending last rep ch 3, join in 3rd ch of beg ch-3.

Rnd 21: Sl st in next 2 dc, *sc in ch-2 shell sp, [ch 5, sc in next lp] 8 times, ch 5, sc in ch-2 shell sp, [ch 5, sc in next lp] 4 times, ch 8, sk next lp, sc in next lp, [ch 6, sc in next lp] 3 times, ch 8, sk next lp, sc in next lp, [ch 5, sc in next lp] 3 times, ch 5, rep from * around, join in first sc.

Rnd 22: Sl st in ch-5 lp, *[4 sc, picot, 4 sc] in 13 ch-5 lps, [5 sc, picot, 5 sc] in next ch-8 lp, [4 sc, picot, 4 sc] in next 3 ch-6 lps, [5 sc, picot, 5 sc] in next ch-8 lp, [4 sc, picot, 4 sc] in next 4 ch-5 lps, rep from * around, join in first sc, fasten off.

—Designed by Melody MacDuffee

Flower Dance

*Seven six-pointed stars with delicate lavender flowers
in the centers form a light and airy doily.*

Getting Started

Experience Level
Beginner

Size
Doily: 12½" in diameter
Each motif: 3¼" in diameter

Materials
- Crochet cotton size 8: 110 yds shaded green, 60 yds light orchid, 55 yds shaded violet, 20 yds cream
- Size 10 steel crochet hook

Gauge
8 sts = ½"

Pattern Note
Join rnds with a sl st unless otherwise stated.

Center Motif

Rnd 1: With light orchid, ch 4, join to form a ring, ch 6, [dc in ring, ch 3] 5 times, join in 3rd ch of beg ch-6.

Rnd 2: Ch 1, [sc, hdc, 3 dc, hdc and sc in ch-3 sp] in each ch-3 sp around, join. (6 petals)

Rnd 3: Ch 1, sc in joining, [ch 5, sc between next 2 sc] 5 times, ch 5, join in beg sc, fasten off.

Rnd 4: Attach shaded violet in any ch-5 sp, ch 1, [sc, hdc, 5 dc, hdc and sc in ch-5 lp] rep in each ch-5 lp around, join.

Rnd 5: Ch 1, sc in joining, [ch 7, sc between next 2 sc] 5 times, ch 7, join in beg sc, fasten off.

Rnd 6: Attach light orchid in any ch-7 lp, ch 1, [sc, hdc, dc, 2 tr, ch 1, 2 tr, dc, hdc and sc in ch-7 lp] rep in each ch-7 lp around, join, fasten off.

Rnd 7: Attach shaded green in ch-1 sp at tip of petal, ch 3 (first dc), 2 dc, ch 2 and 3 dc in same ch-1 sp of petal, ch 7, [shell of 3 dc, ch 2, 3 dc in next ch-1 sp of petal, ch 7] rep around, join.

Rnd 8: Sl st into ch-2 sp of shell, [shell in ch-2 sp of shell, ch 10] 6 times, join.

Rnd 9: Sl st into ch-2 sp of shell, [shell in ch-2 sp of shell, ch 13] 6 times, join.

Rnd 10: Sl st into ch-2 sp of shell, [shell in ch-2 sp of shell, ch 8, sc around ch lp of Rnds 7–9, ch 8] rep around, join, fasten off.

Outer Motifs
Make 6

Rnds 1–9: Rep Rnds 1–9 of Center Motif.

Rnd 10: Join 6 Outer Motifs around Center Motif as follows:

Join at points with neighboring motifs with ch 1, sc in ch-2 sp at point of adjoining motif, ch 1. (This is instead of the ch-2 of a shell.)

Continued on Page 22

Perfect Poinsettias

The perfect doily for placing under your Christmas poinsettia plant,
this festive doily will add a sparkling touch to your winter decor.

Experience Level
Beginner

Size
12" in diameter

Materials
- Crochet cotton size 10: 225 yds white, 50 yds red, 150 yds hunter green
- Size 7 steel crochet hook
- 42 (4mm) yellow beads
- Tapestry needle

Gauge
5 dc = ½"; 3 dc rnds = ¾"

Pattern Note
Join rnds with a sl st unless otherwise stated.

Pattern Stitches
Beaded dc: Yo, insert hook and draw up a lp, move 1 bead close to hook and complete dc. Bead will be on wrong side.

3-dtr cluster (3-dtr cl): *Yo hook 3 times, insert hook and draw up a lp, [yo and draw through 2 lps on hook] 3 times, rep from * 2 more times, yo and draw through all 4 lps on hook.

Hexagon Motifs
Make 7

Rnd 1: With white, ch 6, in 6th ch from hook work [dc, ch 2] 5 times, join in 4th ch of beg ch-6. (6 dc)

Rnd 2: Ch 4 (counts as first dc, ch 1), [5 dc in next dc, ch 1] 5 times, 4 dc in same st as beg dc, join in 3rd ch of beg ch-4. (30 dc)

Rnd 3: Ch 3 (counts as first dc), [3 dc in next dc, dc in each of next 3 dc, 3 dc in next dc] 5 times, 3 dc in next dc, dc in each of next 3 dc, 2 dc in same st as beg ch-3, join in 3rd ch of beg ch-3. (54 dc)

Rnd 4: Ch 3, [2 dc in next dc, dc in each of next 7 dc, 2 dc in next dc] 5 times, 2 dc in next dc, dc in each of next 7 dc, dc in same st as beg ch-3, join in 3rd ch of beg ch-3.

Rnd 5: Ch 6 (counts as first dc, ch 3), *dc in next dc, [ch 1, sk next dc, dc in next dc] 5 times, ch 3, rep from * around, join in 3rd ch of beg ch-3.

Rnd 6: Ch 3, *2 dc in next lp, ch 1, 2 dc in same ch lp, [dc in next dc, dc in next ch sp] 5 times, dc in next dc, rep from * around, join in 3rd ch of beg ch-3, fasten off.

With 1 motif at center, sew 6 rem motifs together around the center motif.

Edging
Rnd 1 (RS): Working around entire outer

edge, attach white to 2nd dc to the left of any joining seam, ch 1, sc in same place, *[ch 4, sk next 2 dc, sc in next dc] 4 times, ch 4, sk next dc, sc in next ch-1 sp, ch 4, sk next dc, sc in next dc, [ch 4, sk 2 dc, sc in next dc] 4 times, ch 4, sk next dc, sc in next ch-1 sp, ch 4, sk next dc, sc in next dc, [ch 4, sk next 2 dc, sc in next dc] 4 times, ch 4, sk ch-1 sp on next motif, sk first dc, sc in next dc, rep from * around, join in top of first dc, fasten off.

Poinsettia

Rnd 1: String 7 beads onto red, ch 1, move 1 bead close to hook, ch 1 to secure, ch 4 (beaded beg dc, ch 2), in first ch worked work [beaded dc, ch 2] 6 times, join in beg ch-1, turn.

Rnd 2 (Petal): Ch 4, work 3-dtr cl in same st, ch 2, sc in top of cl, ch 4, sl st in base of petal, *sl st in ch-2 sp, sl st in next dc, work petal in same place, rep from * around for 4 petals total.

To join next 3 petals to doily, work next petal until cl is made, then ch 1, working in

bottom edge of doily, insert hook in 2nd lp worked on edging, sl st in lp, sc in top of cl, ch 4 and complete petal, sk next lp on doily edging and join next petal in same manner to next lp, sk next lp on doily and join last petal to next lp, fasten off after petal is completed.

Leaves

With Poinsettia at top of doily, sk 2 lps on edging after first petal joined, attach hunter green to next lp, ch 5, work cl in 5th ch from hook, ch 1, insert hook in tip of 4th petal worked on Poinsettia, sl st in tip, sc in top of cl and complete as for petal, [sl st in lp, ch 5, cl in 5th ch from hook, complete as for petal] twice, fasten off.

Work another 3-leaf group in 3rd lp from joining of petal on other side of Poinsettia except join 3rd leaf (instead of first leaf) to next free petal on Poinsettia.

Work 6 Poinsettias with 2 sets of Leaves for each Poinsettia.

—Designed by Rosanne Kropp

Flower Dance

Continued from Page 19

Border

Note: *Each motif has 3 free tips (ch-2 sps of shells) before starting the border.*

Rnd 1: Attach cream in ch-2 sp of any outer point, ch 1, sc in same ch-2 sp, ch 21, [sc in next ch-2 sp of next free point, ch 21] 17 times, join in beg sc.

Rnd 2: Ch 1, sc in same st, 23 sc over ch-21 lp, [sc in next sc, 23 sc over next ch-21 lp] 17 times, join, fasten off.

Rnd 3: Attach shaded violet in any sc at the

center tip of any motif, ch 6, dc in same sp, *[ch 1, sk next sc, dc in next sc] rep to next sc at center tip of next motif, dc, ch 3 and dc in sc at tip, rep from * around, join in 3rd ch of beg ch-6, fasten off.

Rnd 4: Attach cream in any ch-3 sp, ch 1, *in ch-3 sp work sc, ch 3 and sc, sc in each next 17 sts, ch 3, sk 3 sts, [sc in each of next 15 sts, ch 3, sk 3 sts] twice, sc in each of next 17 sts, rep from * around, join, fasten off.

Rnd 5: Attach shaded green in any ch-3 sp, *shell in ch-3 sp, ch 13, [shell in next ch-3 sp, ch 12] twice, shell in next ch-3 sp, ch 13, rep from * around, join.

Rnd 6: Sl st into ch sp of shell, *shell over shell, ch 14, [shell over shell, ch 12] twice, shell over shell, ch 14, rep from * around, join.

Rnd 7: Sl st into ch sp of shell, *shell over shell, ch 15, [shell over shell, ch 12] twice, shell over shell, ch 15, rep from * around, join.

Rnd 8: Sl st into ch sp of shell, *shell over shell, ch 9, sc around ch lp of Rnds 5–7, ch 8, shell over shell, [ch 8, sc around ch lps of Rnds 5–7, ch 8, shell over shell] twice, ch 8, sc around ch lps of Rnds 5–7, ch 9, rep from * around, join, fasten off.

—Designed by Zelda Workman

Craftsmanship

Each time I see the hand of man
At some exalted, noble task,
And watch him work, and scheme, and plan,
There is a question I would ask:

"Is there an art more vital, keen,
Exacting, than the humbler skill
Which brings to life a needed thing—
Some bit o'er which our mothers sing,
And finish with ecstatic thrill?"

A baby bonnet of crochet
To me is just as much a prize
As some cathedral of the day
That thrusts its tower to the skies.

Man's work—his mighty citadels,
His restless boulevards of steel,
His shrines of peace, or battle shells,
His churches, where the weary kneel—

Are these more holy or more fine
Than wee habiliments of youth?
The silk and satin daintiness
Which grace some pretty baby dress;

The crude threads of a thing uncouth.
For, be it lace or rich brocade,
Or peasant stitches, poorly wrought
By faltering fingers—they were made
By loving hands, affection-taught.

Man's cunning gifts, his stalwart deeds,
The empires built, and planets found—
No greater these than humbler needs,
Which never ask to be renowned.

The sewing-basket and the thread;
The needled fabric—these may claim
Immortal grandeur, rise to heights,
As stars are hung on soft, sweet nights,
Yet make no bid for passing fame.

Man never has, and never will
Build finer than the simple thing
Which some dear mother sews, until
The universe is made to sing!

—W. Livingston Larned

Delicate Filet

As a painter creates a masterpiece stroke by careful stroke, so you can create a crochet heirloom stitch by careful stitch. The doilies, runner, centerpiece and place mat included in this collection of vintage filet patterns will provide the perfect accent to an elegant table setting while showcasing your crochet skills.

Winter's First Snowflake

Shadow Rose Doily

Christmas Bells & Holly

Lady's Centerpiece

Diamond Lattice

Winter's First Snowflake

Decorate your home with a touch of winter elegance with this square snowflake doily.
It will fit perfectly under a small dish of candy or vase of fresh flowers.

Getting Started

Experience Level
Beginner

Size
10½" square

Materials
- Crochet cotton size 10 (250 yds per ball): 1 ball white
- Size 9 steel crochet hook

Gauge
12 dc = 1"

Doily

Row 1: Ch 114, dc in 4th ch from hook and in each ch across, ch 3, turn. (112 dc; 37 bls)

Row 2: Sk first dc, dc in each of next 3 dc, *ch 2, sk 2 dc, dc in next dc, rep from * across to last 3 dc, dc in each of last 3 dc (including turning ch), ch 3, turn. (1 bl, 35 sps, 1 bl)

Rows 3–35: Follow graph (Page 33) for design. (Graph shows Rows 1–37.)

Row 36: Sk first dc, dc in each of next 3 dc, *ch 2, sk 2 sts (dc or ch), dc in next dc, rep from * across to last 3 dc, dc in each of last 3 dc, ch 3, turn.

Row 37: Sk first dc, dc in each dc and ch across, turn clockwise to work on side.

Border

Rnd 1: Ch 3, dc in side of last dc on Row 37, ch 2, *dc in side of top of row below, ch 2, rep from * down side to corner, [2 dc, ch 2, 2 dc] in corner, **ch 2, sk 2 dc, dc in base of next dc, rep from ** to next corner, end last rep with ch 2, [2 dc, ch 2, 2 dc] in corner, rep from first * around to last corner, end with 2 dc in corner, ch 1, join with sc in 3rd ch of beg ch-3.

Rnds 2 & 3: Ch 3, dc in same sp, ch 2, sk next dc, *dc in next dc, ch 2, rep from * to corner, dc in first corner dc on Rnd 1, ch 2, [2 dc, ch 2, 2 dc] in corner ch-2 sp, ch 2, sk next dc, dc in last corner dc on Rnd 1, ch 2, rep from * around to last corner ch-2 sp, 2 dc in corner ch-2 sp, ch 1, sc in 3rd ch of beg ch-3.

Rnd 4: Ch 4, 3 dc in corner ch-2 sp, *sc in next ch-2 sp, [2 dc, tr, 2 dc] in next ch-2 sp, rep from * to corner, [2 dc, tr, ch 1, tr, 2 dc] in corner ch-2 sp, rep from first * around to last corner, [3 dc, tr] in last corner sp, ch 1, join in 4th ch of beg ch-4, fasten off.

—Designed by Janice Smallidge

Shadow Rose Doily

From bud to full blossom, roses of every size and color have captured the hearts of people for thousands of years. Capture the elegance of the rose in this beauty.

Getting Started

Experience Level
Intermediate (left-handed)

Size
16" x 20"

Materials
- 4-cord polyester crochet thread (225 yds per ball): 2 balls white
- Size 7 steel crochet hook

Gauge
4 sps = 1"

Pattern Notes

Polyester crochet thread does not shrink when washed; therefore, do not mix with cotton thread or other brands of thread. Cotton threads may be substituted, but must be used throughout.

All sts should be uniform in size, working chs as tightly as possible. Chart rows must be followed from left to right as numbered. ***Note:*** *If right-handed, begin on opposite side of chart.*

Turning ch-3 counts as 1 dc. A turning ch-5 counts as 1 sp.

Special Abbreviations

Sh bl(s): Shadow block(s).

Inc bls: Increase blocks.

Dec bls: Decrease blocks.

Pattern Stitches

Sh bl over sp: After last dc made, ch 1, dc in ch-2 sp, ch 1, dc in next dc.

Sh bl over bl: After last dc made, ch 1, dc between 2nd and 3rd dc of bl, ch 1, dc in next dc.

Sp over sh bl: After last dc made, ch 2, sk ch 1, dc and ch 1, dc in next dc.

Bl over sh bl: Work a dc over each ch-1 and next dc.

Inc bls: Work a dc in bottom side of each extra dc needed (6) for 2 inc bls (see Fig. 1).

Doily

Note: *Do not work foundation ch tightly. If possible, use a larger hook, then change back*

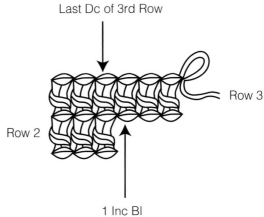

Fig. 1

Last Dc of 3rd Row

Row 3

Row 2

1 Inc Bl
Work 3 more dc for 2 inc bls

to steel crochet hook size 7 to start Row 1.

Row 1: Ch 150 loosely, dc in 4th ch from hook, dc in each of next 2 chs (beg bl made), *ch 2, sk 2 chs, dc in next ch (sp made), dc in each of next 4 chs (bl made), rep from * 23 more times, ch 3, turn. (25 bls and 24 sps)

Row 2: Dc in each of next 3 dc (bl over bl made), *ch 2, sk ch-2 sp, dc in next dc (sp over sp made), dc in each of next 3 dc (bl over bl made), rep from * 23 more times, ch 8, turn. (25 bls and 24 sps)

Row 3: Dc in 4th ch from hook, dc in each of next 4 chs, dc in next dc (2 inc bls made), ch 1, dc between 2nd and 3rd dc of bl, ch 1, dc in last dc of bl (sh bl over bl made), ch 1, dc in ch-2 sp, ch 1, dc in next dc (sh bl over sp made), dc in each of next 3 dc (bl over bl made), ch 1, dc in ch-2 sp, ch 1, dc in next dc (sh bl over sp made), dc in each of next 3 dc (bl over bl made), *ch 2, sp over sp, bl over bl, rep from * 19 more times, sh bl over sp, bl over bl, 2 sh bls (1 over a sp and 1 over a bl), 2 inc bls to end row, ch 5, turn. (4 inc bls, 6 sh bls, 23 bls and 20 sps)

Row 4: Sk 2 dc, dc in next dc (beg sp made), ch 2, sp over sp, 2 sh bls, bl, sh bl, [bl, sp] 20 times, bl, sh bl, bl, 2 sh bls, 2 sps, ch 3, turn.

Row 5: 5 bls, sh bl, [bl, sp] 20 times, bl, sh bl, 5 bls, ch 5, turn.

Row 6: 2 sps, 4 sh bls, [bl, sp] 20 times, bl, 4 sh bls, 2 sps, ch 3, turn.

Row 7: 6 bls, 2 sps, bl, [3 sps, bl] 3 times, [sp, bl] twice, [3 sps, bl] twice, [sp, bl] twice, [3 sps, bl] twice, 2 sps, 6 bls, ch 5, turn.

Rows 8–63: Follow chart on Page 31 (rows must be worked back and forth) until Row 63 has been completed, ch 1 tightly to turn.

Row 64: Sl st across next 7 dc (do not sk last dc of Row 63), ch 3, [dc over ch-1 sp] twice, dc in next dc (beg bl made), ch 2, sk sh bl, dc in next dc (sp over sh bl made), dc in each of next 3 dc, *sp, bl, rep from * 23 times, ch 3, turn. (25 bls and 24 sps)

Row 65: Dc in each of next 3 dc (beg bl made), [sp, bl] 24 times, do not fasten off or turn.

Edging

Note: *If right-handed, beg edging at opposite end of Row 65 (see Fig. 2 on Page 32).*

Rnd 1: Sc in last dc worked (Row 65), *ch 1, tr in center of "L" formed by 2 vertical and 2 horizontal rows of doily, [ch 1, tr in same place] 2 more times, ch 1, sc in side of last dc, ch 3 *, [4 dc in next sp, ch 2] rep until 29 bls are completed (long side completed), ch 3, sc in side of last dc row, rep from * to * for 2nd corner, [4 dc in next sp, ch 2] rep until 24 bls are completed (short side completed); finish 3rd corner, long side, 4th corner and short side to correspond, ending with ch 3, join in first sc.

Rnd 2: Sl st in ch-1 and in next tr, ch 6, [tr, ch 3, tr] in next tr (center), ch 1, tr in next tr, ch 2, [dc, ch 1, dc, ch 1, dc] in ch-3 sp, ch 4 (corner started), *4 dc in next ch-2 sp, ch 3, [dc, ch 1, dc] in next ch-2 sp, ch 3 *, rep from * to * 13 more times, 4 dc in next ch-2 sp (side completed), ch 4, [dc, ch 1, dc, ch 1, dc] in ch-3 sp, ch 2, tr in next tr, ch 1, [tr, ch 3, tr] in next tr, ch 1, tr in next tr, ch 2, [dc, ch 1, dc, ch 1, dc] in next ch-3 sp, ch 4 (2nd corner completed), rep from * 3 more times, ending with ch 4, [dc, ch 1, dc, ch 1, dc] in next ch-3 sp, ch 2, join in 4th ch of beg ch-6.

Rnd 3: Ch 1, sc in joining, ch 7, sl st in 4th ch from hook (picot made), ch 3, sc in next ch-3 sp at corner, ch 7, picot in 4th ch from hook, [ch 5, picot in 4th ch] twice, ch 3, sc in same ch-3 sp, ch 7, picot in 4th ch from hook, ch 3, sc in next tr, ch 7, picot as before, ch 3, sc in 2nd dc of 3-dc group, ch 7, picot, ch 3, sc in next ch-4 sp (beg corner made),

Right-handers begin edging here,
working down bottom
after working first corner

Side

Left-handers begin
edging here; edging
worked in this direction

Row 65

Row 65

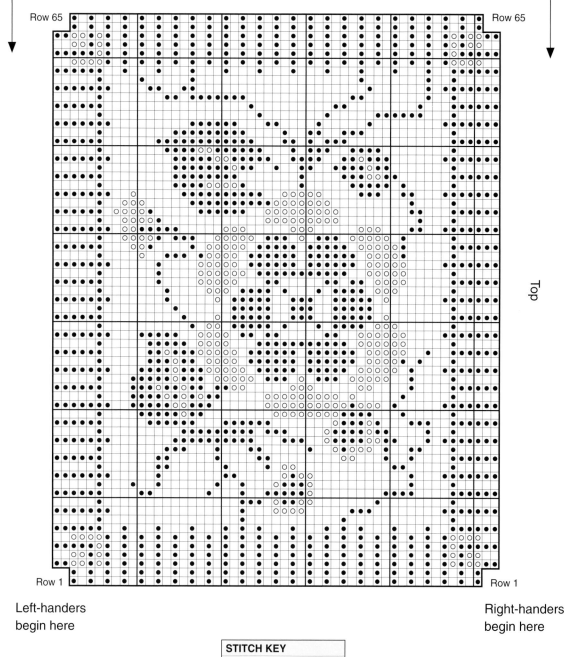

Top

Row 1

Row 1

Left-handers
begin here

Right-handers
begin here

STITCH KEY

◉	Bl
☐	Sp
◉	Sh bl

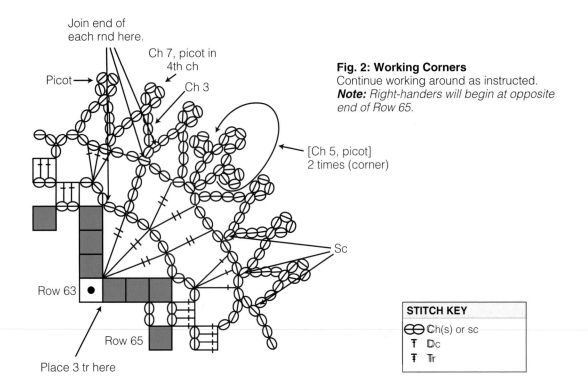

Join end of
each rnd here.

Ch 7, picot in
4th ch

Ch 3

Picot →

Fig. 2: Working Corners
Continue working around as instructed.
Note: *Right-handers will begin at opposite
end of Row 65.*

[Ch 5, picot]
2 times (corner)

Sc

Row 63 ●

Row 65

Place 3 tr here

STITCH KEY	
⊖⊖	Ch(s) or sc
⊤	Dc
⊤	Tr

*ch 7, picot, ch 3, sc in next ch-3 sp, [2 dc, ch 3, picot in top of last dc worked, dc, ch 3, picot as before, dc] in next ch-1 sp *, rep from * to * down side, end with ch-7, picot, ch 3, sc in ch-4 sp.

2nd corner: **Ch 7, picot, ch 3, sc in 2nd dc of dc group, ch 7, picot, ch 3, sc in first tr, ch 7, picot, ch 3, sc in next ch-3 sp, ch 7, picot, [ch 5, picot in 4th ch from hook] twice, ch 3, sc in same sp, ch 7, picot, ch 3, sc in last tr, ch 7, picot, ch 3, sc in 2nd dc of dc group, ch 7, picot, ch 3, sc in next ch-4 sp **.

Rep from * to * to complete remaining sides.

Rep from ** to ** in 2nd corner to complete corners.

To complete beg corner, ch 7, picot, ch 3, sc in 2nd dc of dc group, ch 7, picot, ch 3, join in sc of first picot lp, fasten off.

—Designed by Tomi Alderman

Winter's First Snowflake

Continued from Page 27

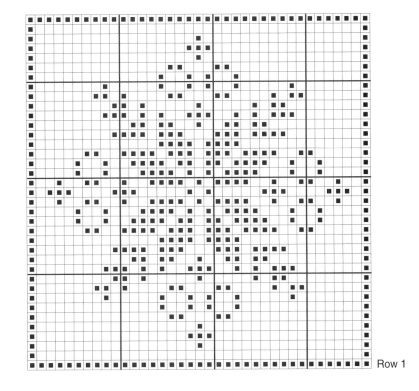

Row 1

Winter's Snow

Snowing, snowing everywhere
Far as the eye can see;
It covers all the grass and streets,
And hangs upon the trees.

It's Nature's way of telling us
The earth does need a rest;
It worked hard all summer long
To please ourselves at best,

So now it's sleeping silently
Underneath the snow,

To return again in springtime
To give us all a show.

The rains will come so silently
And wash away the white;
Another winter's come and gone,
And days are getting bright.

So feast your eyes upon the snow,
Enjoy it when you can.
A world of white is a glorious sight,
Just ask any man.

—Mildred Winkler

Christmas Bells & Holly

Greet the holiday season and guests with a set of enchanting Christmas place mats. Try crocheting a set in red or green and placing over a white tablecloth for an especially festive look!

Getting Started

Experience Level
Beginner

Size
11½" x 16"

Materials
- Crochet cotton size 10: 250 yds white
- Size 6 steel crochet hook

Gauge
20 mesh and 16 rows = 4"

Place Mat

Row 1: Ch 147, dc in 4th ch from hook, dc in each rem ch across, turn.

Rows 2 & 3: Ch 3, dc in each of next 2 dc, [ch 1, sk 1 dc, dc in next dc] rep across to last 3 sts, dc in each of last 2 dc, dc in 3rd ch of beg ch-3, turn.

Row 4: Ch 3, dc in each of next 2 dc, following graph, [ch 1, sk 1 dc, dc in next dc] for open mesh, [dc in ch-1 sp, dc in next dc] for solid sps. Each square on graph represents 1 mesh.

Rows 5–47: Complete Place Mat following graph. Fasten off at end of Row 47.

—Designed by Carolyn Christmas

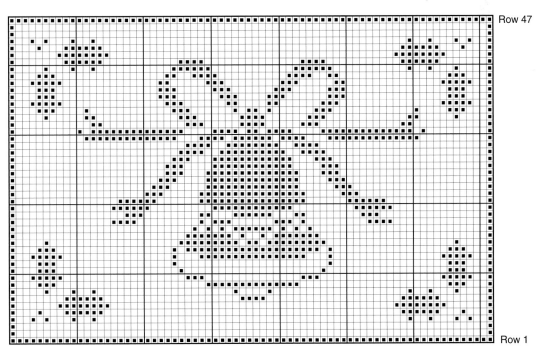

Row 47

Row 1

Lady's Centerpiece

Adorn any bureau or dresser with this elegant oblong centerpiece.
It is the perfect place for setting a treasured jewelry box or family photo.

Getting Started

Experience Level
Intermediate

Size
16½" x 34"

Materials
- Crochet cotton size 20: 900 yds white
- Size 9 steel crochet hook

Gauge
12 dc = 1"; 5 dc rows = 1"

Pattern Notes

To dec at the beg of a row, sl st to beg st as indicated on graph on Page 41.

To dec at the end of a row, end at indicated bl on graph.

To inc at the beg of a row, ch 7, dc in last dc of previous row.

To inc at the end of a row, ch 5, dc in same last dc of row, sl st in 3 chs.

Beg foundation ch is the center of centerpiece.

Centerpiece

First Half
Row 1: Ch 212, dc in 8th ch from hook, *[ch 2, sk 2 chs, dc in next ch] 17 times, dc in each of next 6 chs, [ch 2, sk 2 chs, dc in next ch] 5 times, dc in each of next 57 chs, [ch 2, sk 2 chs, dc in next ch] 5 times, dc in each of next 6 chs, [ch 2, sk 2 chs, dc in next ch] 18 times, ch 5 (counts as first dc, ch 2 of following row), turn. (18 sps, 2 bls, 5 sps, 19 bls, 5 sps, 2 bls and 18 sps)

Rows 2–79: Follow graph (Page 41), working sps and bls as indicated.

At end of Row 79, fasten off.

Second Half
Row 1: Attach cotton in first ch of opposite side of foundation ch, ch 5 (counts as first dc, ch 2), sk 2 chs, dc in next ch, rep from * of Row 1 of first half.

Rows 2–79: Follow graph, working sps and bls as indicated.

At end of Row 79, do not fasten off.

Edging
Rnd 1: Ch 1, sc evenly sp around, working 2 sc in each point for fullness needed to make centerpiece lie flat, join in beg ch-1, fasten off.

—Designed by Dorothy Newman

Diamond Lattice

These pretty diamonds are worked in a lovely lattice-style design. A delicate openwork edging finished off with dainty scallops completes this perfect piece.

Getting Started

Experience Level
Beginner

Size
21" x 29"

Materials
- Crochet cotton size 10: 700 yds white
- Size 2 steel crochet hook

Gauge
Work evenly and consistently throughout

Pattern Notes

A block (bl) is shown as a ● on the graph (Page 40) and consists of 3 dc. When 1 bl stands alone there will be 4 dc in the group, the first of which belongs to the previous sp. When 2 bls stand alone there will be 7 dc in the group, 3 for each bl and 1 for the previous sp. Therefore, all groups of bls will have 3 times as many dcs as there are ●s, plus 1 dc.

When working the bl into a sp, work the first 2 dc into the sp and the 3rd dc into the next dc.

A sp is shown as an open square on the graph and consists of 2 chs, sk 2 chs or 2 dc, 1 dc into next dc for each sp.

Ch 3 at beg of each row counts as first dc throughout unless otherwise indicated.

Join rnds with a sl st unless otherwise stated.

Runner

Row 1: Ch 162, dc in 4th ch from hook, dc in each rem ch across, turn. (160 dc)

Row 2: Ch 3, dc in each of next 3 dc, [ch 2, sk 2 dc, dc in next dc] 51 times, dc in each of next 2 dc, dc in 3rd ch of beg ch-3, turn.

Rows 3–95: Follow graph for remainder of runner. At the end of Row 95, do not fasten off.

Border

Rnd 1: *Working down side, ch 5, sc in top of next row, [ch 5, sk 1 row, sc in top of next row] rep down side to corner, ch 7, sk 2 dc, sc in next dc st for corner, [ch 7, sk 5 dc, sc in next dc] rep across bottom, rep corner, rep from * across rem 2 sides of runner, join.

Rnd 2: Sl st into center of ch-5 sp, [ch 7, sc in center of next ch-5 sp] rep around, join.

Rnd 3: Sl st to center of ch-7 sp, ch 3, 1 dc, ch 3, 2 dc in ch-7 sp, work shell of 2 dc, ch 3, 2 dc in each ch-7 sp around, with 2 dc, ch 3, 2 dc, ch 3, 2 dc in each corner ch-7 sp, join.

Rnd 4: Sl st to ch-3 sp of beg shell, ch 3, 9 dc in ch-3 sp, *sc in ch-3 sp of next shell, 10 dc in ch-3 sp of next shell, rep from * for pattern to corner, corner sp has 2 ch-3 sps, 2 dc, ch 3, 2 dc in first ch-3 sp at corner, 2 dc, ch 3, 2 dc in 2nd ch-3 sp of corner, resume pattern starting with 10 dc in ch-3 sp of next shell st, rep from * around rem sides, join, fasten off.

—Designed by Glenda Winkleman

Lady's Centerpiece

See instructions on Page 37

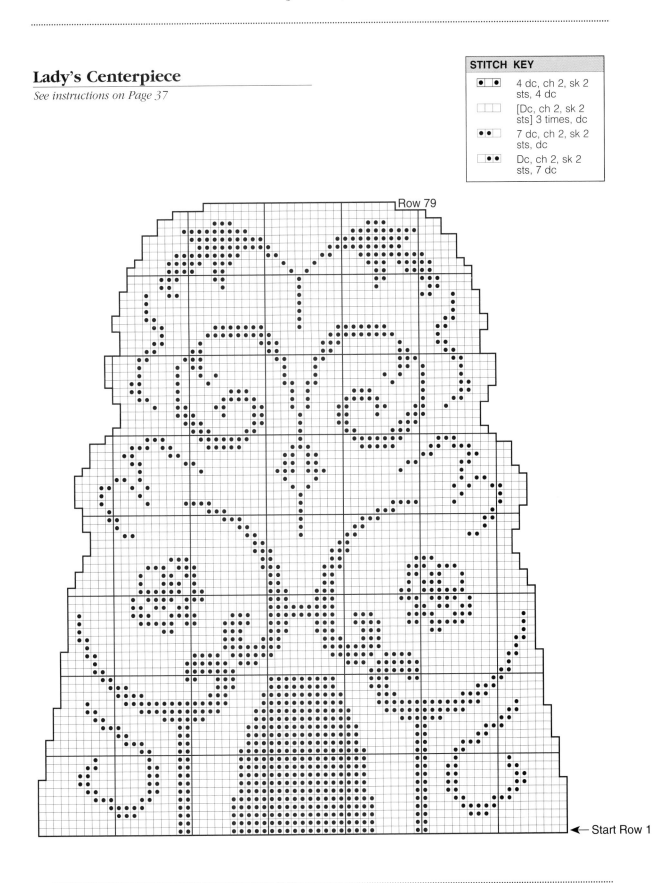

Row 79

← Start Row 1

Versatile Motifs

Motifs are a favorite among crocheters because of their wonderful versatility and delicate, lacy look. Each of the exquisite motifs in this chapter, from dainty flowers to elegant stars, can be crocheted together into doilies, tablecloths, bedspreads, runners and even vests. Custom-make your own heirloom design to suit your personal decor and style.

Delicate Snowflakes

Julie Anne Tablecloth

Starflower Doily

Gem Clusters

Starlit Serenade

Delicate Snowflakes

These easy, six-pointed motifs can be crocheted into doilies, runners and tablecloths of different shapes and sizes to perfectly accent your decor.

Getting Started

Experience Level
Beginner

Size
Motif: 3" from shell to shell
Diamond Doily: 13½" x 21½"
Round Doily: 8½" in diameter

Materials
- Crochet cotton size 30: 550 yds white
- Size 10 steel crochet hook

Gauge
4 dc = ¼"; 1 dc rnd = ¼"

Pattern Notes

Materials listed will make 1 Diamond Doily and 2 Round Doilies.

When making a larger doily or tablecloth, keep in mind each motif requires approximately 11 yards of crochet cotton. Allow sufficient cotton for edging.

Join rnds with a sl st unless otherwise stated.

Motifs

First Motif

Rnd 1: Ch 4, join in first ch to form a ring, ch 2, 11 hdc in ring, join in 2nd ch of beg ch-2. (12)

Rnd 2: Ch 5 (counts as 1 dc, ch 2), [dc in next hdc, ch 2] rep around, join in 3rd ch of beg ch-5.

Rnd 3: Sl st into ch-2 sp, ch 3, dc, ch 3, 2 dc in ch-2 sp, ch 2, dc in next ch-2 sp, ch 2, [shell of 2 dc, ch 3, 2 dc in next ch-2 sp, ch 2, dc in next ch-2 sp, ch 2] rep around, join in 3rd ch of beg ch-3.

Rnd 4: Sl st into ch-3 sp of shell, ch 3, 2 dc, ch 3, 3 dc in ch-3 sp, ch 3, dc in single dc between shells, ch 3, [shell of 3 dc, ch 3, 3 dc in ch-3 sp of shell, ch 3, dc in single dc between shells, ch 3] rep around, join in 3rd ch of beg ch-3.

Rnd 5: Sl st into ch-3 sp of shell, ch 3, 3 dc, ch 3, 4 dc in ch-3 sp, ch 4, dc in single dc between shells, ch 4, [shell of 4 dc, ch 3, 4 dc in ch-3 sp of shell, ch 4, dc in single dc between shells, ch 4] rep around, join in 3rd ch of beg ch-3.

Rnd 6: Sl st into ch-3 sp of shell, ch 3, 4 dc, ch 3, 5 dc in ch-3 sp, ch 4, dc in single dc between shells, ch 4, [shell of 5 dc, ch 3, 5 dc in ch-3 sp of shell, ch 4, dc in single dc between shells, ch 4] rep around, join in 3rd ch of beg ch-3, fasten off.

Second Motif

Rnds 1–5: Rep Rnds 1–5 of First Motif.

Rnd 6: Sl st into ch-3 sp of shell, ch 3, 4 dc, ch 3, 5 dc in ch-3 sp, ch 4, dc in single dc between shells, ch 4, [shell of 5 dc, ch 3, 5 dc in ch-3 sp of shell, ch 4, dc in single dc between

Continued on Page 49

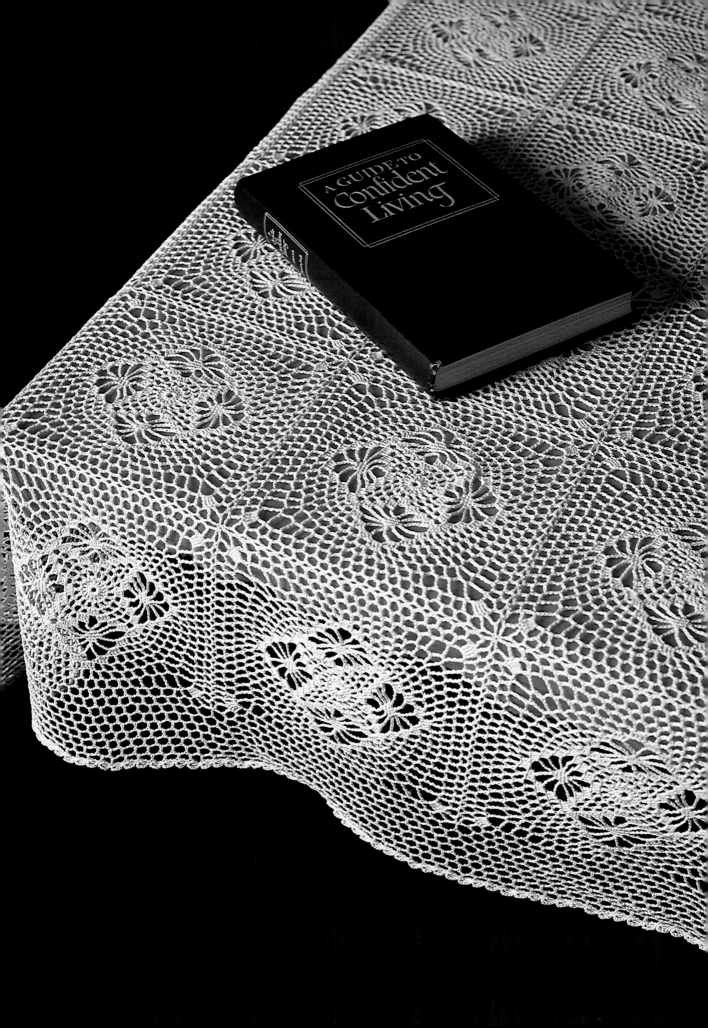

Julie Anne Tablecloth

Eye-catching, lacy centers set off the square motifs
of this elegant tablecloth suited to formal dining.

Pattern Note
Join rnds with a sl st unless otherwise stated.

Motifs
Make 88

First Motif

Rnd 1: Ch 6, join in first ch to form a ring, ch 4 (counts as first dc, ch 1), [dc in ring, ch 1] 15 times, join in 3rd ch of beg ch-4. (16 dc)

Rnd 2: Ch 5 (counts as first dc, ch 2), [dc in next dc, ch 2] rep around, join in 3rd ch of beg ch-5. (16 dc)

Rnd 3: Ch 5, dc in next dc, ch 2, dc in next dc, *ch 2, dc in next ch-2 sp, 2 dc in next dc, dc in next ch-2 sp, [ch 2, dc in next dc] 3 times, rep from * around, join in 3rd ch of beg ch-5.

Rnd 4: Ch 5, dc in next ch-2 sp, ch 2, dc in next ch-2 sp, *ch 2, dc in next dc, 2 dc over next ch-2 sp, dc in next dc (block made), ch 7, sk 2 dc, dc in next dc, 2 dc over ch-2 sp, dc in next dc, [ch 2, dc in next ch-2 sp] twice, rep from * around, join in 3rd ch of beg ch-5.

Rnd 5: Ch 3, *2 dc in next ch-2 sp, dc in next dc, ch 2, dc in next ch-2 sp, ch 2, dc in next dc, 2 dc in next ch-2 sp, dc in next dc, ch 5, sc in next ch-7 lp, ch 5, sk 3 dc, dc in next dc, rep from * around, join in 3rd ch of beg ch-3.

Rnd 6: Sl st into last (4th) dc of block, ch 3, *3 dc in ch-2 sp, ch 2, 3 dc in next ch-2 sp, dc in next dc, ch 6, sc in ch-5 lp, sc in next sc, sc in next ch-5 lp, ch 6, sk 3 dc, dc in next dc, rep from * around, join in 3rd ch of beg ch-3.

Rnd 7: Sl st into last (4th) dc of block, ch 3, *[3 dc, ch 2, 3 dc] in next ch-2 sp, dc in next dc, ch 7, sc in next ch-6 lp, sc in each of next 3 sc, sc in ch-6 lp, ch 7, sk 3 dc, dc in next dc, rep from * around, join in 3rd ch of beg ch-3.

Rnd 8: Ch 5 (counts as first dc, ch 2), *sk 1 dc, dc in next dc, ch 2, dc over ch-2 lp, ch 2, sk 1 dc, dc in next dc, ch 2, sk 1 dc, dc in next dc, 3 dc over ch-7 lp, ch 7, sk 1 sc, sc in each of next 3 sc, ch 7, 3 dc over ch-7 lp, dc in next dc, ch 2, rep from * around, join in 3rd ch of beg ch-5.

Rnd 9: Sl st into next lp, ch 5, [dc in next

lp, ch 2] 3 times, *[ch 2, sk 1 dc, dc in next dc] twice, 3 dc in ch-7 lp, ch 7, sk 1 sc, sc in next sc, ch 7, 3 dc in ch-7 lp, dc in next dc, ch 2, sk 1 dc, dc in next dc, [ch 2, dc in next ch-2 lp] 4 times, rep from * around, join in 3rd ch of beg ch-5.

Rnd 10: Sl st into next lp, ch 6, dc in next lp, *[ch 3, dc in next lp] 3 times, [ch 3, sk 1 dc, dc in next dc] twice, 3 dc in ch-7 lp, ch 2, 3 dc in next ch-7 lp, dc in next dc, ch 3, sk 1 dc, dc in next dc, [ch 3, dc in next lp] 4 times, rep from * around, join in 3rd ch of beg ch-6.

Rnd 11: Sl st in next lp, ch 6, dc in next lp, [ch 3, dc in next lp] 4 times, *[ch 3, sk 1 dc, dc in next dc] twice, 2 dc over next ch-2 sp, dc in next dc, ch 3, sk 1 dc, dc in next dc, [ch 3, dc in next lp] 10 times, rep from * around, join in 3rd ch of beg ch-6.

Rnd 12: Sl st in next lp, ch 9, *tr in same lp, ch 3, tr in next lp, [ch 3, dc in next lp] 5 times, ch 3, dc in next dc, ch 3, sk 2 dc, dc in next dc, [ch 3, dc in next lp] 5 times, [ch 3, tr in next lp] twice, ch 5, rep from * around, join in 4th ch of beg ch-9.

Rnd 13: Sl st into next lp, ch 10, dtr in same lp, *ch 3, dtr in next lp, [ch 3, tr in next lp] twice, [ch 3, dc in next lp] 9 times, [ch 3, tr in next lp] twice, [ch 3, dtr in next lp] twice, ch 5, dtr in same lp, rep from * around, join in 5th ch of beg ch-10.

Rnd 14: Ch 6, *4 tr in ch-5 lp, ch 3, dc in next dtr, [ch 3, dc in next lp] 16 times, ch 3, dc in next dtr, ch 3, rep from * around, join in 3rd ch of beg ch-6.

Rnd 15: Sl st into ch-3 lp, ch 6, sk 1 tr, tr in next tr, ch 5, tr in next tr, *[ch 3, dc in next sp] 19 times, ch 3, sk 1 tr, tr in next tr,

ch 5, tr in next tr, rep from * around, join in 3rd ch of beg ch-6, fasten off.

Second & Subsequent Motifs

Rnds 1–14: Rep Rnds 1–14 of First Motif.

Note: *Attach motifs to each other in the 15th rnd by placing motifs back to back and working Rnd 15.*

Rnd 15: Sl st into next lp, ch 6, sk 1 tr, tr in next tr, ch 2, sl st into center of matching ch-5 lp between trs on previous motif, ch 2, tr in next tr, *[ch 1, sl st into center of next ch-3 lp of previous motif, ch 1, dc in next sp on working motif] 19 times, ch 1, sl st into center of next ch-3 lp of previous motif, ch 1, sk 1 tr, tr in next tr on working motif, ch 2, sl st into center of matching ch-5 lp between trs on previous motif, ch 2, tr in next tr, complete as for previous motif, fasten off.

Join 88 motifs in an 8 x 11 motif configuration or as desired.

Border

Rnd 1: Attach thread in any joining between motifs, ch 6, *dc in next ch-3 sp, ch 3, rep from * until you reach the next joining between motifs, dc in joining, rep in this fashion around, except work corners with dc, ch 5, dc in same lp, ending join in 3rd ch of beg ch-6.

Rnd 2: Sl st into next ch-3 sp, ch 6, [dc in next sp, ch 3] rep around, with [dc, ch 5, dc] in each corner ch-5 lp, ending join in 3rd ch of beg ch-6.

Rnds 3–7: Rep Rnd 2.

Rnd 8: *Ch 5, dc in same sp, sl st into next dc (picot), rep from * around, with 3 picots in each corner, join to base of beg ch-5, fasten off.

—Designed by Linda May Rude

Delicate Snowflakes

Continued from Page 45

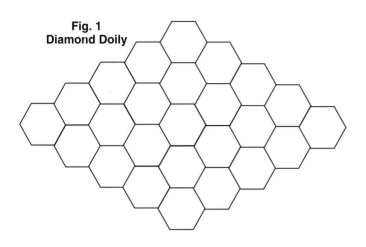

**Fig. 1
Diamond Doily**

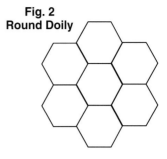

**Fig. 2
Round Doily**

shells, ch 4] 3 times, to join to previous motif, *5 dc in next ch-3 sp, ch 1, sl st in ch-3 sp of shell of previous motif, ch 1, 5 dc in same ch-3 sp, ch 4, dc in single dc between shells, sl st in dc opposite on previous motif, ch 4 *, rep from * to * once, join in 3rd ch of beg ch-3, fasten off.

Subsequent Motifs

Continue working motifs by repeating Rnds 1–5 of First Motif, working Rnd 6 as in Second Motif, joining as needed to previous motifs. As work progresses, you will be joining 3 and sometimes 4 shells as in Rnd 6 from * to *.

Diamond Doily

Diamond Doily requires 25 motifs. Follow Fig. 1 for placement.

Round Doily

Each Round Doily requires 7 motifs. Follow Fig. 2 for placement.

Edging

Rnd 1: Attach cotton in any ch-3 sp of single shell (2 shells that are joined in the ch-3 sps is different), ch 1, [sc, ch 5, sc in ch-3 sp, ch 5, sk 4 dc of shell, sc in next dc, ch 5, sk ch-4 sp, sc in next dc, ch 5, sk ch-4 sp, sc in next dc of shell, ch 5] rep around, [except at point where 2 shells are joined from joining the motifs, ch 5, sk 4 dc of shell, sc in next ch-3 sp of shell, sc in next ch-3 sp of shell, ch 5, sk 4 dc, sc in next dc of shell] rep around, join.

Rnd 2: Sl st into ch-5 sp, ch 1, work 7 sc in each ch-5 sp around, join, fasten off.

—Designed by Agnes Russell

Starflower Doily

Each of these small, delicate floral motifs is quick and easy to make. Join them together to make a doily, tablecloth or bedspread in any size or shape desired.

Experience Level
Beginner

Size
18½" from point to point

Materials
- Crochet cotton size 8: 150 yds shaded yellow, 150 yds white, 50 yds bright yellow
- Size 10 steel crochet hook

Gauge
Each starflower measures 1⅛" in diameter

Pattern Note
Join rnds with a sl st unless otherwise stated.

Center Motif
Make 1

Rnd 1: With white, ch 6, join in first ch to form a ring, ch 6 (counts as first dc, ch 3), [dc in ring, ch 3] 5 times, join in 3rd ch of beg ch-6.

Rnd 2: In each ch-3 sp work sl st, ch 4, 3 tr, ch 4, sl st (1 petal), join, fasten off.

Remaining Motifs
Make 54 more white flowers, as follows, working both rnds with white. Make 72 yellow flowers, as follows, by working Rnd 1 with bright yellow and Rnd 2 with shaded yellow.

Rnd 1: Ch 6, join in first ch to form a ring, ch 6 (counts as first dc, ch 3), [dc in ring, ch 3] 5 times, join in 3rd ch of beg ch-6.

Note: *Flowers are joined together in Rnd 2 as work progresses. Use diagram on Page 59 as a guideline for joining and color of individual starflowers.*

Rnd 2 (Joining Rnd): In ch-3 sp of Rnd 1 work [sl st, ch 4, 2 tr], ch 1, sl st in center tr of adjoining petal, ch 1, sl st in top of last tr made on working flower, tr in same ch-3 sp, ch 4, sl st in same ch-3 sp.

Press doily; do not starch.

—Designed by Zelda Workman

Gem Clusters

*Set the mood for a romantic dinner for two
with this beautiful, draping tablecloth.*

Getting Started

Experience Level
Intermediate

Size
58" square (11 x 11 motifs)

Materials
- Crochet cotton size 10: 3,200 yds ecru
- Size 9 steel crochet hook

Gauge
Finished square: 5½" square

Pattern Note
Join rnds with a sl st unless otherwise stated.

Pattern Stitches
Tr cluster (tr cl): *Yo hook twice, insert hook in tr, draw up a lp, [yo, draw through 2 lps on hook] twice, rep from * 4 more times, yo, draw through all 6 lps on hook.

3-tr cluster (3-tr cl): *Yo hook twice, insert hook in st, draw up a lp, [yo, draw through 2 lps on hook] twice, rep from * 2 more times in same st, yo, draw through all 4 lps on hook.

Motifs
Make 121

First Motif
Rnd 1: Ch 6, join to form a ring, ch 5 (counts as first dc, ch 2), [1 dc in ring, ch 2] 7 times, join in 3rd ch of beg ch-5. (8 dc)

Rnd 2: Ch 1, sc in same st, 3 sc in next ch-2 sp, [sc in next dc, 3 sc in next ch-2 sp] rep around, join in beg sc. (32 sc)

Rnd 3: Ch 1, sc in same st as beg ch-1, [ch 9, sk 3 sc, sc in next sc] 7 times, ch 5, sk 3 sc, join with dtr in beg sc.

Rnd 4: Ch 1, sc, ch 5 and sc in same st as beg ch-1, [ch 9, sc, ch 5 and sc in 5th ch of next ch-9 sp] 7 times, ch 5, join with dtr in beg sc.

Rnd 5: Ch 1, sc in same st as beg sc, ch 11, [sc in 5th ch of ch-9, ch 11] 7 times, join in beg sc.

Rnd 6: Ch 1, sc in same st as beg sc, ch 5, [tr, ch 3 and tr] in 6th ch of ch-11, ch 5, [sc in next sc, ch 5, {tr, ch 3 and tr} in 6th ch of ch-11, ch 5] rep around, join in beg sc.

Rnd 7: Sl st across to first tr, ch 4 (counts as first tr), 3 tr in ch-3 sp, tr in next tr, ch 7, sc in next sc, ch 7, [tr in tr, 3 tr in ch-3 sp, tr in tr, ch 7, sc in next sc, ch 7] rep around, join in 4th ch of beg ch-4.

Rnd 8: Ch 4, [tr cl over 5 tr, ch 5, sl st in first ch of ch-5 for picot, ch 7, tr in 4th ch of ch-7 sp, ch 3, tr in 4th ch of ch-7 sp, ch 7] rep around, join in top of beg tr cl, fasten off. (8 ch-5 picots around motif)

Second & Subsequent Motifs
Rnd 1–7: Rep Rnds 1–7 of First Motif.

Continued on Page 58

Starlit Serenade

A constellation of star motifs creates this delicate, lacy tablecloth to share with your guests the beauty of the night sky.

Getting Started

Experience Level
Advanced

Size
Tablecloth: 54" x 72"
Motif: approximately 4" square unblocked

Materials
- 100 percent mercerized crochet cotton size 20 (300 yds per ball): 24 balls white
- Size 10 steel crochet hook

Gauge
6 dc = ½"; 3 dc rnds = ½"

Pattern Notes
Tablecloth consists of 21 rows, alternating 13 and 12 motifs each, plus border.

Join rnds with a sl st unless otherwise stated.

Motifs
Make 263

First Motif
Rnd 1: Ch 5, join to form a ring, ch 3, work 17 dc in ring, join in 3rd ch of beg ch-3.

Rnd 2: Ch 3, work 2 dc in next dc, *ch 3, sk 1 dc, dc in next dc, 2 dc in next dc, rep from * around, ending ch 3, join in 3rd ch of beg ch-3.

Rnd 3: Ch 3, 2 dc in next dc, dc in next dc, *ch 4, dc in next dc, 2 dc in next dc, dc in next dc, rep from * around, ending ch 4, join in 3rd ch of beg ch-3.

Rnd 4: Ch 3, dc in next dc, ch 3, dc in each of next 2 dc, dc in ch-4 sp, *ch 3, dc in ch-4 sp, dc in each of next 2 dc, ch 3, dc in each of next 2 dc, dc in ch-4 sp, rep from * around, ending ch 3, dc in ch-4 sp, join in 3rd ch of beg ch-3.

Rnd 5: Ch 6, sc in ch-3 sp, ch 3, sk 1 dc, dc in each of next 2 dc, dc in ch-3 sp, *ch 3, dc in ch-3 sp, dc in each of next 2 dc, ch 3, sc in next ch-3 sp, ch 3, sk 1 dc, dc in each of next 2 dc, dc in ch-3 sp, rep from * around, ending ch 3, dc in ch-3 sp, dc in next dc, join in 3rd ch of beg ch-6.

Rnd 6: Sl st into ch-3 sp, ch 1, sc in same sp, *ch 5, sc in next ch-3 sp, ch 3, sk 1 dc, dc in each of next 2 dc, dc in ch-3 sp, ch 3, dc in ch-3 sp, dc in each of next 2 dc, ch 3, sc in next ch-3 sp, rep from * around, ending ch 3, join in beg sc.

Rnd 7: Sl st to center of ch-5, ch 1, sc in same sp, *ch 3, dc in ch-3 sp, dc in each of next 2 dc, ch 3, sc in next ch-3 sp, ch 3, sk 1 dc, dc in each of next 2 dc, dc in ch-3 sp, ch 3, sc in ch-5 sp, rep from * around, join in first sc.

Rnd 8: Sl st across to last ch-3 sp, ch 3, dc in each of next 2 dc, *ch 3, sc in ch-3 sp, ch 5, sc in next ch-3 sp, ch 3, sk 1 dc, dc in each of next 2 dc, dc in ch-3 sp, ch 2, dc in next ch-3 sp, dc in each of next 2 dc, rep from * around, ending ch 2, join in 3rd ch of beg ch-3.

Rnd 9: Ch 3, dc in next dc, *ch 3, sc in ch-3 sp, [ch 6, sc in next ch lp] twice, ch 3, sk 1 dc, dc in each of next 2 dc, 2 dc in ch-2 sp, dc in each of next 2 dc, rep from * around, ending 2 dc in ch-2 sp, join in 3rd ch of beg ch-3.

Rnd 10: Ch 6, *sc in ch-3 sp, [ch 6, sc in next ch lp] 3 times, ch 3, sk 1 dc, dc in each of next 4 dc, ch 3, rep from * around, ending ch 3, sk 1 dc, dc in each of next 3 dc, join in 3rd ch of beg ch-6.

Rnd 11: Sl st into ch-3 sp, ch 1, sc in same sp, *[ch 7, sc in next ch lp] 4 times, ch 3, sk 1 dc, dc in next dc, ch 5, sl st in top of last dc (picot), dc in next dc, ch 3, sc in next ch lp, rep from * around, ending ch 3, join in first sc, fasten off.

Subsequent Motifs

Rnds 1–10: Rep Rnds 1–10 of First Motif for all subsequent motifs.

Note: Use these directions for all subsequent motifs on every side where the motif is attached to another motif.

Place motifs to be attached back to back.

Rnd 11 (joining rnd): Beg attaching at any picot; after the first dc in picot, ch 2, sl st into center of matching picot on motif you are joining to, ch 2, sl st in top of last dc worked, dc in next dc, ch 3, sc in next lp, *ch 3, sc into ch of matching ch-7 lp on the motif you are joining, ch 3, sc in next lp] 4 times, ch 3, sk 1 dc, dc in next dc, ch 2, sl st into center of picot of motif you are joining to, ch 2, sl st in top of last dc, dc in next dc.

Join in this fashion on all sides necessary, joining the motifs in hexagon fashion. At end of rnd, join, fasten off.

Border

Begin on even edge.

Rnd 1: Beg in any picot in the center on the even edge, attach thread, ch 1, sc in same sp, *[ch 7, sc in next lp] 2 times, ch 7, hdc in next lp, ch 7, dc in next lp, ch 7, tr in top of 2 dc of picot, ch 7, sk joining of motifs, tr in top of 2 dc of next picot, ch 7, dc in next lp, ch 7, hdc in next lp, [ch 7, sc in next lp] twice, ch 7, sc in next picot, rep from * until you reach the first free picot of corner motif.

Corner Instructions

Rnd 1: [Ch 7, sc in next lp] twice, ch 7, hdc in next lp, ch 7, dc in next lp, ch 7, tr in picot, ch 7, dc in next lp, ch 7, hdc in next lp, [ch 7, sc in next lp] twice, ch 7, sc in next picot.

Uneven Edge

Rnd 1: *[Ch 7, sc in next lp] twice, ch 7, hdc in next lp, ch 7, dc in next lp, [tr in top of 2 dc of next picot] twice, dc in next ch-7 lp, [ch 5, dc in next lp] 3 times, tr in top of 2 dc of picot and tr in top of 2 dc of 2nd picot, dc in next lp, ch 7, hdc in next lp, [ch 7, sc in next lp] twice, ch 7, sc in next picot, [ch 7, sc in next lp] 4 times, ch 7, sc in next picot, rep from * across side to 2nd free picot of next corner motif.

Turn next corner as before, work next even edge as previous, turn corner in same fashion, work uneven edge in same fashion, turn last corner in same manner and work rem portion of first even edge as before, ending ch-3, tr in first sc.

Even Edge

Rnd 2: Ch 1, sc in same sp, *[ch 7, sc in next lp] 3 times, ch 7, hdc in next lp, ch 7, dc in next lp, ch 7, tr in next lp, ch 7, dc in next lp, ch 7, hdc in next lp, [ch 7, sc in next lp] 3 times, rep from * around until you reach the lp before the picot on the corner motif. Place a marker in the last lp worked.

Corner Instructions

Rnd 2: [Ch 7, sc in next lp] twice, ch 7, hdc in next lp, ch 7, dc in next lp, ch 7, tr in next lp, ch 7, tr in tr, ch 7, tr in next lp, ch 7, dc in next lp, ch 7, hdc in next lp, [ch 7, sc in next lp] twice. Place a marker in last lp worked.

Uneven Edge

Rnd 2: *Ch 7, sc in next lp, ch 7, hdc in next lp, ch 7, dc in next lp, ch 7, tr in next lp, sk next 2 tr and tr in next lp, ch 4, tr in next lp, ch 4, tr in next lp, sk next 2 tr and tr in next lp, ch 7, dc in next lp, ch 7, hdc in next lp, [ch 7, sc in next lp] 6 times, rep from * across, ending with last lp before first picot in corner motif. Place marker in last lp worked.

Continue to work in this fashion around, placing markers in the last lp of each section and ending with ch 3, tr in first sc.

Even Edge

Rnd 3: Ch 1, sc in same sp, *[ch 7, sc in next lp] 4 times, ch 7, hdc in next lp, [ch 7, dc in next lp] twice, ch 7, hdc in next lp, [ch 7, sc in next lp] 3 times, rep from * across to lp with marker. Replace marker in last lp worked.

Corner Instructions

Rnd 3: [Ch 7, sc in next lp] 3 times, ch 7, hdc in next lp, ch 7, dc in next lp, ch 7, tr in next lp, ch 7, dtr in tr, ch 7, tr in next lp, ch 7, dc in next lp, ch 7, hdc in next lp, [ch 7, sc in next lp] twice. Replace marker in last lp worked.

Uneven Edge

Rnd 3: *Ch 7, sc in next lp, ch 7, hdc in next lp, ch 7, dc in next lp, ch 7, [tr in next lp] twice, ch 4, [tr in next lp] twice, ch 7, dc in next lp, ch 7, hdc in next lp, [ch 7, sc in next lp] 5 times, rep from * across, ending at marked lp. Replace marker in last lp worked.

Work in the same fashion around, ending ch 3, tr in first sc.

Even Edge

Rnd 4: Ch 1, sc in same sp, *ch 7, sc in next lp, rep from * to marker. Do not replace marker.

Corner Instructions

Rnd 4: [Ch 7, sc in next lp] 7 times, ch 9, sc in next lp, [ch 7, sc in next lp] 4 times. Place marker in last lp worked.

Uneven Edge

Rnd 4: *Ch 7, sc in next lp, ch 7, hdc in next lp, ch 7, dc in next lp, ch 7, tr in next lp, sk 1 lp, tr in next lp, ch 7, dc in next lp, ch 7, hdc in next lp, [ch 7, sc in next lp] 4 times, rep from * across until you reach marker.

Continue working in the same fashion around, ending with ch 3, tr in first sc.

Even Edge

Rnd 5: Ch 1, sc in same lp, *ch 7, sc in next lp, rep from * across to corner ch-9 lp, ch 7, sc in same lp.

Uneven Edge

Rnd 5: Ch 1, sc in next lp, *[ch 7, sc in next lp] 4 times, ch 7, hdc in next lp, ch 7, dc in next lp, [ch 7, tr in next lp] twice, ch 7, dc in next lp, ch 7, hdc in next lp, rep from * across side, into next corner lp, ch 7, sc in same lp.

Continue in this fashion around, ending ch 3, tr in first sc.

Even Edge

Rnd 6: Ch 1, sc in same sp, *ch 7, sc in next lp, rep from * across until corner lp, ch 7, sc in same lp.

Uneven Edge

Rnd 6: [Ch 7, sc in next lp] 6 times, *ch 7,

hdc in next lp, ch 7, dc in next lp, ch 7, tr in next lp, ch 7, dc in next lp, ch 7, hdc in next lp, [ch 7, sc in next lp] 5 times, rep from * until corner lp, ch 7, sc in same lp.

Continue around in this fashion, ending ch 3, tr in first sc.

Even Edge

Rnd 7: Ch 1, sc in same sp, *ch 7, sc in next lp, rep from * until corner lp, ch 7, sc in same lp.

Uneven Edge

Rnd 7: [Ch 7, sc in next lp] 4 times, *ch 7, hdc in next lp, [ch 7, dc in next lp] 8 times, ch 7, hdc in next lp, rep from * across, ending ch 7, sc in next lp until the

corner lp, ch 7, sc in same lp.

Work in same fashion around, ending ch-3, tr in first sc.

Even Edge

Rnd 8: Ch 1, sc in same sp, *ch 7, sc in next lp, rep from * until corner lp, ch 7, sc in same lp.

Uneven Edge

Rnd 8: [Ch 7, sc in next lp] 3 times, *[ch 8, sc in next lp] 4 times, [ch 9, sc in next lp] 6 times, rep from * across until 3 lps from corner lp, [ch 7, sc in next lp] 3 times, ch 7, sc in same lp.

Continue around in this fashion, ending ch 7, join in first sc, fasten off.

—Designed by Linda May Rude

Gem Clusters

Continued from Page 53

Rnd 8: Rep Rnd 8 of First Motif, joining working motif to previous motif at picots, ch 2, sl st in ch-5 picot of previous motif, ch 2, sl st in base of beg ch-2, join, fasten off.

Fill-in Motifs
Make 100

Note: *Fill-in motifs are attached in opening between motifs.*

Rnds 1–3: Rep Rnds 1–3 of First Motif.

Rnd 4: Ch 4, 3-tr cl in same st as beg ch-4, ch 2, sl st in joining of motifs, ch 2, sl st in first ch of first ch-2 to form picot, ch 9, sc in 5th ch of next ch-9, ch 9, [3-tr cl in 5th ch of next ch-9, ch 2, sl st in joining of motifs, ch 2, sl st in first ch of first ch-2 to form picot, ch 9, sc in

5th ch of next ch-9, ch 9] rep around, join in top of beg cl, fasten off.

Edging

Rnd 1: Attach cotton in 3rd picot of any corner motif, ch 4, 4 tr in same picot, ch 7, tr in tr, 3 tr in ch-3 sp, tr in tr, ch 7, 5 tr in next picot, ch 7, tr in tr, 3 tr in ch-3 sp, ch 9, tr in tr on next motif, 3 tr in ch-3 sp, tr in tr, ch 7, 5 tr in picot, continue to rep basic pattern around, join in 4th ch of beg ch-4.

Rnd 2: Ch 4, tr cl over 5 tr, ch 5, sl st in first ch of ch-5 for picot, *ch 7, sc in 4th ch of ch-7, ch 7, tr cl over 5 tr, picot, rep from * twice, ch 5, sc in 5th ch of ch-9, ch 5, tr cl over 5 tr, ch 7, tr cl over 5 tr, continue to rep basic pattern around, join in base of first picot, fasten off.

—Designed by Gloria Coombes

Starflower Doily

See instructions on Page 51

COLOR KEY

W = White starflowers
All other flowers are yellow

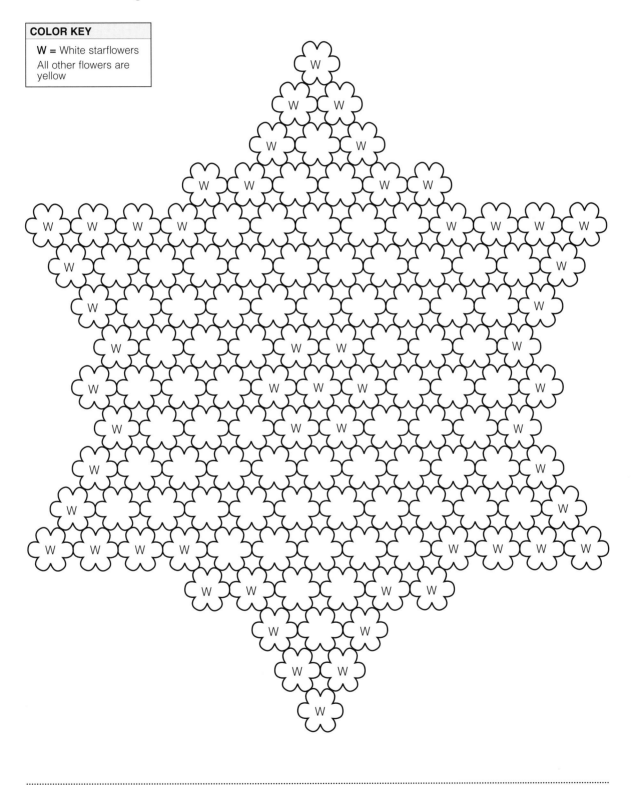

Grandma's Attic

Visiting Grandma's house as a child was always an anticipated adventure. Discovering dusty books and photographs, playing around heavy, antique furniture and smelling Grandma's newest treat from the oven were common to us all. Relive those fond memories by first browsing through this chapter of treasured doilies from Grandma's attic, and finally, creating your own version for your grandchildren to admire!

Oval Rose Doily

Christmas Ruffles

Antique Lace

Sunburst Ruffle

Irish Morn

Oval Rose Doily

Worked in a soft rose color, this attractive doily makes a pretty accent for your living room, dining room or bedroom.

Getting Started

Experience Level
Intermediate

Size
12½" x 15½"

Materials
- Crochet cotton size 10 (150 yds per ball): 2 balls rose
- Size 4 steel crochet hook

Gauge
9 dc = 1"

Pattern Note
Join rnds with a sl st unless otherwise stated.

Pattern Stitches

2-tr cluster (2-tr cl): *Yo twice, insert hook through sp, yo, draw thread through sp, [pull thread through 2 lps on hook] twice, rep from * once, yo, draw thread through all lps on hook.

3-tr cluster (3-tr cl): Follow instructions for 2-tr cl and rep from * twice.

4-dc cluster (4-dc cl): *Yo hook, insert hook through sp, draw thread through sp, yo, draw thread through 2 lps on hook, rep from * 3 times, yo, draw thread through all lps on hook.

5-dc cluster (5-dc cl): Follow instructions for 4-dc cl and rep from * 4 times.

Doily

Rings: Ch 30, join to form a ring, fasten off. Rep for 2 more rings, passing the ch through previous ring before joining with a sl st. Do not fasten off after forming 3rd ring, ch 3.

Rnd 1: Work 49 dc in first ring, join in 3rd ch of first ch-3, fasten off.

Rep Rnd 1 for 2nd and 3rd rings, do not fasten off at end of 3rd ring.

Rnd 2: Ch 4, [sk next dc, dc in next dc, ch 2] 5 times, {sk next dc, holding next ring and current ring tog, dc in next dc through both thicknesses, ch 2}, rep bet [] 5 times, rep between {} once, rep bet [] 18 times, rep bet {} once, rep bet [] 5 times, rep between {} once, rep bet [] 11 times, join in 3rd ch of beg ch-4. (50 ch-2 sps)

Rnd 3: Ch 3 (counts as first dc), 4-dc cl in same sp, ch 3, *5-dc cl, ch 3 in next sp, rep from * around, join in 3rd ch of beg ch-3. (50 cls)

Rnd 4: Ch 3 (counts as 1 dc), 2 dc in same sp, *3 dc in next sp, rep from * around, join in 3rd ch of beg ch-3.

Rnd 5: *Ch 5, sk next dc, sl st in next dc, rep from * around, join in first sl st.

Rnds 6–8: Sl st in each of next 2 chs, *ch 5,

Continued on Page 67

Christmas Ruffles

Two pretty ruffles make this centerpiece doily especially festive. Use it to set off a bowl of Christmas candies or a lovely poinsettia during the holiday season.

Getting Started

Experience Level
Advanced

Size
26" in diameter

Materials
- Crochet cotton size 10: 600 yds white, 400 yds red and 300 yds hunter green
- Size 8 steel crochet hook

Gauge
8 dc = 1"; 3 dc rnds = 1"

Pattern Notes

When attaching a new color, attach with a sl st in same stitch where old color was fastened off unless otherwise indicated.

Join rnds with a sl st unless otherwise stated.

Pattern Stitch

Tr cluster (tr cl): 3 tr in same sp holding back the last lp of each tr on hook, yo, pull through all rem lps on hook.

Doily

Rnd 1: With white cotton, ch 4, join to form a ring, ch 1, 8 sc in ring, join. (8 sc)

Rnd 2: Ch 3, dc in same st, [ch 2, 2 dc in next st] 7 times, ch 2, join in 3rd ch of beg ch-3. (16 dc)

Rnd 3: Ch 3, dc in same dc, 2 dc in next dc, ch 2, [2 dc in each of next 2 dc, ch 2] 7 times, join in 3rd ch of beg ch-3. (32 dc)

Rnd 4: Sl st into next dc, ch 3, dc in next dc, [ch 2, dc in ch-2 sp, ch 2, sk next dc, dc in next 2 dc] 7 times, ch 2, dc in ch-2 sp, ch 2, join in 3rd ch of beg ch-3, fasten off.

Rnd 5: Attach hunter green, ch 6 (counts as 1 dc, ch 3), dc in next dc, ch 3, [dc in next dc, ch 3] rep around, join in 3rd ch of beg ch-6.

Rnd 6: Ch 3, 3 dc in next ch-3 sp, [dc in next dc, 3 dc in ch-3 sp] rep around, join in 3rd ch of beg ch-3, fasten off. (96 dc)

Rnd 7: Attach white, ch 5 (counts as 1 dc, ch 2), [sk next dc, dc in next dc, ch 2] rep around, join in 3rd ch of beg ch-5, fasten off.

Rnd 8: Attach red, ch 6 (counts as 1 dc, ch 3), [dc in next dc, ch 3] rep around, join in 3rd ch of beg ch-6.

Rnd 9: Ch 3, 2 dc in next sp, [dc in next dc, 2 dc in next sp] rep around, join in 3rd ch of beg ch-3, fasten off. (144 dc)

Rnd 10: Attach white, ch 5 (counts as 1 dc, ch 2), [sk next dc, dc in next dc, ch 2] rep around, join in 3rd ch of beg ch-5.

Rnd 11: Ch 1, sc in same st, work 1 sc in each ch sp and 1 sc in each dc around, join, fasten off.

Rnd 12: Attach hunter green and working in back lps for this rnd only, ch 3, dc in each of next 11 sts, ch 3, [dc in each of next 12 sts, ch 3] rep around, join in 3rd ch of beg ch-3.

Rnd 13: Sl st to next dc, ch 3, dc in each of next 9 dc, ch 3, dc in next ch-3 sp, ch 3, [sk next dc, dc in each of next 10 dc, ch 3, dc in next ch sp, ch 3] rep around, join in 3rd ch of beg ch-3.

Rnd 14: Sl st to next dc, ch 3, dc in each of next 7 dc, ch 3, [dc in next ch sp, ch 3] twice, *sk next dc, dc in each of next 8 dc, ch 3, [dc in next ch sp, ch 3] twice, rep from * around, join.

Rnd 15: Sl st to next dc, ch 3, dc in each of next 5 dc, ch 3, [dc in next ch sp, ch 3] 3 times, *sk next dc, dc in each of next 6 dc, ch 3, [dc in next ch sp, ch 3] 3 times, rep from * around, join.

Rnd 16: Sl st to next dc, ch 3, dc in each of next 3 dc, ch 3, [dc in next ch sp, ch 3] 4 times, *sk next dc, dc in each of next 4 dc, ch 3, [dc in next ch sp, ch 3] 4 times, rep from * around, join.

Rnd 17: Sl st to next dc, ch 3, dc in next dc, ch 3, [dc in next ch sp, ch 3] 5 times, *sk next dc, dc in each of next 2 dc, ch 3, [dc in next ch sp, ch 3] 5 times, rep from * around, join.

Rnd 18: Sl st to center of next ch sp, ch 7 (counts as 1 dc, ch 4), [dc in next ch lp, ch 4] rep around, join in 3rd ch of beg ch-7.

Rnd 19: Ch 3, 3 dc in next ch sp, [dc in next dc, 3 dc in ch sp] rep around, join in 3rd ch of beg ch-3, fasten off. (288 dc)

Rnd 20: Attach white, rep Rnd 10.

Rnd 21: Rep Rnd 11, fasten off.

Rnd 22: Attach red with a sl st in 8th sc to right of where white was fastened off, ch 3, dc in each of next 11 sc, ch 3, [dc in each of next

12 sc, ch 3] rep around, join in 3rd ch of beg ch-3. (24 groups of 12 dc)

Rnds 23–28: Rep Rnds 13–18. Fasten off at the end of Rnd 28.

Outer Ruffle

Rnd 29: Attach white, ch 5, dc in same sp, ch 2, dc in next dc, ch 2, [dc in next sp, ch 2, dc in same sp, ch 2, dc in next dc, ch 2] rep around, join in 3rd ch of beg ch-5.

Rnd 30: Sl st to center of next ch sp, ch 6, [dc in next ch sp, ch 3] rep around, join in 3rd ch of beg ch-6.

Rnd 31: Sl st to center of next ch sp, ch 7, [dc in next ch sp, ch 4] rep around, join in 3rd ch of beg ch-7.

Rnd 32: Sl st to center of next ch sp, ch 8, [dc in next ch sp, ch 5] rep around, join in 3rd ch of beg ch-8.

Rnd 33: Sl st to center of next ch sp, ch 9, [dc in next ch sp, ch 6] rep around, join in 3rd ch of beg ch-9.

Rnd 34: Sl st to center of next ch sp, ch 10, [dc in next ch sp, ch 7] rep around, join in 3rd ch of beg ch-10.

Rnd 35: Sl st to center of next ch sp, ch 11, [dc in next ch sp, ch 8] rep around, join in 3rd ch of beg ch-11, fasten off.

Rnd 36: Attach red with a sl st in next sp after where white was fastened off, ch 12, [dc in next sp, ch 9] twice, tr cl in next sp, *[ch 9, dc in next ch sp] 8 times, ch 9, tr cl in next sp, rep from * around, join in 3rd ch of beg ch-12, fasten off.

Inner Ruffle

Rnd 1: Attach white with a sl st in any rem free lp of Rnd 11, ch 5, [dc in next lp, ch 2] rep around, join in 3rd ch of beg ch-5.

Rnds 2–5: Rep Rnds 30–33 of Outer Ruffle. Fasten off at the end of Rnd 5.

Rnd 6: Attach hunter green in next ch sp, ch 10, [dc in next sp, ch 7] rep around, join in 3rd ch of beg ch-10, fasten off.

Finishing

To finish doily, follow Ruffled Doilies finishing instructions under General Instructions on Page 152.

—Designed by Colleen Sullivan

Oval Rose Doily

Continued from Page 63

Continued from Page 63

sl st in 3rd ch of next ch-5 sp, rep from * around, join in beg sl st.

Rnd 9: Sl st in next sp, ch 3, 2 dc in same sp, *3 dc in next sp, rep from * around, join in 3rd ch of beg ch-3.

Rnd 10: *Ch 4, 2-tr cl in same dc, sk next 6 dc, 2-tr cl in next dc, ch 5, sl st in same dc, rep from * around, join in 4th ch of beg ch-4.

Rnd 11: *Ch 4 (counts as first tr), 2-tr cl in same sp, ch 6, 3-tr cl in same sp, *3-tr cl between the next cls of previous rnd, ch 6, 3-tr cl in same sp, rep from * around, join in 4th ch of beg ch-4.

Rnd 12: Ch 3 (counts as first dc), 8 dc in same sp, *9 dc in next sp, rep from * around, join in 3rd ch of beg ch-3.

Rnds 13–16: Rep Rnds 5–8.

Rnd 17: Rep Rnd 9.

Rnd 18: *Ch 6, sk next 5 dc, sl st in next dc, rep from * around.

Rnd 19: *[Sc, hdc, 5 dc, hdc, sc] in next sp (scallop made), rep from * around, join in first sc.

Rnd 20: Sl st in each of next 3 sts, *ch 6, sl st in 3rd dc of next scallop, rep from * around, join in first ch of beg ch-6.

Rnd 21: Rep Rnd 19, fasten off.

—Designed by Nazanin S. Fard

Grandmother has a hymn-book with great silver clasps, and she often reads in that book; in the middle of the book lies a rose, quite flat and dry; it is not as pretty as the roses she has standing in the glass; and yet she smiles at it most pleasantly of all, and tears even come into her eyes. I wonder why Grandmother looks at the withered rose in the old book that way?

—— Hans Christian Andersen (1805–1875), Danish Writer

Antique Lace

This dainty doily includes seven small hexagons surrounded by pretty lace flowers.
Place it under a vase of fresh flowers for a beautiful antique look.

Getting Started

Experience Level
Advanced beginner

Size
Doily: 12" in diameter
Motif: 2¼" in diameter

Materials
- Crochet cotton size 10 (225 yds per ball): 1 ball ecru
- Size 7 steel crochet hook

Gauge
5 sc = ½"

Pattern Note
Join rnds with a sl st unless otherwise stated.

Hexagon Motif
Make 7

Rnd 1: Ch 4, join to form a ring, ch 5 (counts as 1 dc, ch 2), [dc in ring, ch 2] 5 times, join in 3rd ch of beg ch-5.

Rnd 2: Ch 4, dc in same st, 3 dc in next ch-2 sp, [dc, ch 1, dc in next dc, 3 dc in next ch-2 sp] rep around, join in 3rd ch of beg ch-4.

Rnd 3: Sl st into ch-1 sp, ch 4, dc in same ch-1 sp, *[ch 1, sk next dc, dc in next dc] twice, ch 1, sk next dc, dc, ch 1, dc in next ch-1 sp, rep from * around, join in 3rd ch of beg ch-4.

Rnd 4: Sl st into ch-1 sp, ch 4, dc in same ch-1 sp, [dc in next dc, dc in next ch-1 sp] 3 times, dc in next dc, *dc, ch 1, dc in ch-1 sp, [dc in next dc, dc in ch-1 sp] 3 times, dc in next dc, rep from * around, join.

Rnd 5: Ch 1, [sc in each dc, 2 sc in each ch-1 sp] rep around, fasten off.

Joining
Sew motifs together, with 1 in the center and the rem 6 around the outer edge of the center motif.

Large Flowers
Make 6

Center Ring
Rnd 1: Ch 10, join to form a ring, ch 1, work 15 sc in ring, join.

Three Large Petals
Row 2: Ch 17, sc in 4th ch from hook, ch 1, [sk 1 ch, hdc in next ch, ch 1] twice, [sk 1 ch, dc in next ch, ch 1] 3 times, ch 1, sk 2 chs, sl st in next ch, ch 2, turn.

Row 3: [Dc in top of dc, sk ch-1, ch 1] 3 times, [sk ch-1, hdc in next hdc, ch 1] twice, sc in sc, work 3 sc in tip of leaf, sc in each st and in each ch-1 sp down side of leaf, work 3 sc in ch-2 sp, sl st at base of leaf, turn.

Row 4: Sc in each sc side of leaf, 2 sc in center sc at tip of leaf, sc in each ch-1 sp and in each st down other side of leaf, 3 sc in ch-2 sp,

Continued on Page 75

Sunburst Ruffle

This beautiful doily features a lovely swirl pattern in the center surrounded by pretty pleats. Crocheted with yellow thread, it brings sunshine inside.

Experience Level
Beginner

Size
15½" in diameter

Materials
- Crochet cotton size 10: 2 balls each white, sunshine yellow and shaded yellow
- Size 7 steel crochet hook

Gauge
Work evenly and consistently throughout

Pattern Notes
Do not join rnds unless otherwise stated.

Join rnds with a sl st where indicated.

Doily
Rnd 1: With yellow, ch 8, join to form a ring, *ch 5, sc in ring, rep from * 4 times.

Rnd 2: Ch 2, 3 sc in first lp, *ch 6, 3 sc in next lp, rep from * 3 times.

Rnd 3: *Ch 6, sk next sc, sc in each of next 2 sc, 3 sc in next lp, rep from * 4 times.

Rnd 4: *Ch 6, sk 1 sc, sc in each sc, 3 sc in next lp, rep from * 4 times.

Rnds 5–11: Rep Rnd 4, always skipping the first sc of each sc group and working 3 sc in each lp.

Rnd 12: *Ch 6, sk 2 sc, sc in each of next 18 sc, ch 6, sc in next lp, rep from * 4 times.

Rnd 13: *Ch 6, sk 2 sc, sc in each of next 15 sc, ch 6, sc in next lp, ch 6, sc in next lp, rep from * 4 times.

Rnd 14: *Ch 6, sk 2 sc, sc in each of next 12 sc, [ch 6, sc in next lp] 3 times, rep from * 4 times.

Rnd 15: *Ch 6, sk 2 sc, sc in each of next 9 sc, [ch 6, sc in next lp] 4 times, rep from * 4 times.

Rnd 16: *Ch 6, sk 1 sc, sc in each of next 7 sc, [ch 6, sc in next lp] 5 times, rep from * 4 times.

Rnd 17: Ch 4, sk 1 sc, dc in next sc, [ch 2, sk 1 sc, dc in next sc] twice, ch 4, sc in next lp, [ch 6, sc in next lp] 5 times, rep from beg 3 times, ch 4, sk 1 sc, dc in next sc, ch 2, sk 1 sc, dc in next sc, ch 2, sk 1 sc, dc in next sc, ch 4, sc in next lp, [ch 6, sc in next lp] 4 times.

Rnd 18: Ch 5, dc in next lp, [ch 3, dc in next lp] 3 times, ch 5, sc in next lp, [ch 6, sc in next lp] 4 times, rep from beg 4 times, ending last rep with ch 2, dc in center of first lp (this brings thread in position for next rnd).

Rnd 19: Ch 12, sc in same lp where last dc was worked, *ch 12, sc in next lp, rep from * around, ending ch 12, join.

Rnd 20: [Ch 1, 17 sc] over each lp, join.

Rnd 21: Ch 1, working in back lps, *sc in

Continued on Page 74

Irish Morn

This elegant eye-catcher was originally designed in 1944. Amidst the world crisis of that time, the unknown designer found time and peace to create a lovely work of art.

Getting Started

Experience Level
Advanced

Size
10" in diameter

Materials
- Crochet cotton size 30 (450 yds per ball): 1 ball white
- Size 12 steel crochet hook

Gauge
Work evenly and consistently throughout

Pattern Note
Join rnds with a sl st unless otherwise stated.

Doily

Rnd 1: Ch 12, join to form a ring, ch 1, 24 sc in ring, join in first sc.

Rnd 2: Ch 1, sc in same place, *ch 25, sc in 2nd ch from hook, hdc in each of next 2 chs, dc in each of next 2 chs, tr in each of next 14 chs, dc in each of next 2 chs, hdc in each of next 2 chs, sc in next ch, sc in each of next 2 sc, rep from * around, end last rep sc in sc, join in first sc, fasten off. (12 spokes)

Rnd 3: Attach thread in 14th ch of ch-25 (count from base of spoke), ch 1, sc in same place, *sc in each of next 5 sts, ch 3, sc in 3rd ch from hook (picot), sc in each of next 5 sts,

[ch 3, sc in 3rd ch from hook] 3 times, sc in same st as last sc before picots, sc in each of next 4 sts, picot, sc in each of next 6 sts, picot, sc in 14th ch of next spoke, rep from * around, end last rep picot, join in first sc.

Rnd 4: Sl st in each of next 4 sc and in first ch of picot, sl st in picot, ch 5, picot, ch 2, picot, ch 1, sc in center picot at tip of spoke, *ch 1, picot, ch 2, picot, ch 1, [sk next picot, tr in next picot] twice, ch 1, picot, ch 2, picot, ch 1, sk next picot, sc in next picot at tip of spoke, rep from * around, join last tr to 4th ch of beg ch-5.

Rnd 5: Sl st to sp between next 2 picots, ch 10, *dc between picots of next lp, ch 7, rep from * around, end ch 7, join in 3rd ch of beg ch-10. (24 sps)

Rnd 6: Sl st in ch-7 sp, ch 1, [sc, hdc, 7 dc, hdc, sc] in each ch-7 sp around, join in first sc. (24 petals)

Rnd 7: *Ch 2, picot, ch 3, picot, ch 2 (picot lp), sc in center dc of petal, picot lp, sc between petals, rep from * around, join in first sc. (48 picot lps)

Rnds 8–11: Sl st to center of next picot lp, ch 1, sc in same place, *picot lp, sc between picots of next picot lp, rep from * around, join in first sc.

Rnd 12: Sl st to center of next picot lp, ch 10, *dc in center of next picot lp, ch 7, rep from * around, join in 3rd ch of beg ch-10.

Rnd 13: Rep Rnd 6. (48 petals)

Rnd 14: Sl st to center dc of next petal, ch

1, sc in same place, *picot lp, sc in center dc of next petal, rep from * around, end with picot lp, join in first sc.

Rnd 15: Sl st to center of next picot lp, ch 1, sc in same place, *[picot lp, sc in center of next picot lp] 3 times, ch 7, sc in center of next picot lp, ch 1, turn, 9 sc over ch-7 just made, ch 1, turn, sc in each of 9 sc just made, rep from * around, join in first sc.

Rnd 16: Sl st to center of next picot lp, ch 1, sc in same place, *[picot lp, sc in center of next picot lp] twice, ch 2, picot, ch 1, dc in next sc, [ch 2, sk next sc, dc in next sc] 4 times, turn, [sc, hdc, dc, hdc, sc] in each of next 4 ch-2 sps, ch 1, turn, sc in each of next 20 sts, ch 1, picot, ch 2, sc in center of next picot lp, rep from * around, join in first sc.

Rnd 17: Sl st to center of next picot lp, ch 1, sc in same place, *ch 7, sc in center of next picot lp, ch 1, turn, 9 sc over ch-7 just made, ch 1, turn, sc in next 9 sc, [picot lp, sc in center dc of next shell] 4 times, picot lp, sc in center of next picot lp, rep from * around, join in first sc on first scallop.

Rnd 18: Ch 5, *[sk next sc, dc in next sc, ch 2] 3 times, dc in last sc, turn, [sc, hdc, dc, hdc, sc] in each of next 4 ch-2 sps, ch 1, turn, sc in each of next 20 sts, ch 1, picot, ch 2, sc in center of next picot lp, [picot lp, sc in center of next picot lp] 4 times, ch 2, picot, ch 1, dc in next sc, ch 2, rep from * around, end ch 2, picot, ch 1, join in 3rd ch of beg ch-5.

Rnd 19: Sl st to center dc of next shell, ch

1, sc in same place, *[ch 7, sc in center dc of next shell] 3 times, ch 7, sc in center of next picot lp, [picot lp, sc in center of next picot lp] 3 times, ch 7, sc in center dc of next shell, rep from * around, join last ch-7 in first sc.

Rnd 20: Ch 1, 11 sc in each of next 3 ch-7 lps, 6 sc in next ch-7 lp, turn, [ch 7, sc in center sc of next lp] 3 times, ch 1, turn, 12 sc in each of next 3 lps, 5 sc in remainder of next ch-7 lp, *ch 2, picot, [tr, picot] 4 times between picots of next 3 picot lps, ch 2, 11 sc in each of next 4 ch-7 lps, 6 sc in next ch-7 lp, turn, [ch 7, sc in center sc of next lp] 4 times, ch 1, turn, 12 sc in each of next 4 lps, 5 sc in remainder of next ch-7 lp, rep from * around, end 11 sc in last ch-7 lp, sl st in base of first lp, sl st to center of same lp, ch 7, turn, sc in center st of last lp, ch 1, turn, 12 sc over ch-7 just made, join in first sc, fasten off.

Rosette

Rnd 1: Ch 10, join to form a ring, ch 1, 20 sc in ring, join in first sc.

Rnd 2: Ch 1, sc in same place, *ch 5, sk next 3 sc, sc in next sc, rep from * around, end last rep ch 5, sl st in first sc. (5 ch-5 lps)

Rnd 3: Sl st in lp, [sc, hdc, 5 dc, hdc, sc] in each ch-5 lp around, join in first sc.

Rnd 4: *Ch 5, sc in sp between next 2 petals, rep from * around, join in base of first ch-5.

Rnd 5: Sl st in lp, [sc, hdc, 7 dc, hdc, sc] in each ch-5 lp around, join in first sc, fasten off.

Sew Rosette to center of doily. ❖

Sunburst Ruffle

Continued from Page 71

each of next 7 sc, 3 sc in next sc, sc in each of next 7 sc, sk 2 sc, rep from * around, join.

Rep the last rnd for remainder of doily, working 14 more rnds yellow, 4 rnds shaded yellow and 4 rnds white, join.

—Designed by Linda McMahon

Antique Lace

Continued from Page 69

sc in same st on ring as this leaf was started, sc in next 2 sc on Rnd 1 of center ring.

Rep Rows 2–4 twice more for 2 more large petals, then continue on to small petals.

Two Small Petals

Rnd 1: *Ch 10, turn, sl st in same st, ch 1, turn, 1 sc, 2 hdc, 3 dc, 2 tr, 3 dc, 2 hdc and 1 sc all in the ch-10 lp, sc in same st on ring as lp was started. Sc in next 2 sc on Rnd 1 of center ring, sl st in next sc. Rep from * once more.

Joining

Sew the large flowers to points of motifs, sewing only the 2 small petals to edges. If desired, join flowers as crocheted as follows: On small petals, join at the tr sts by working st until 2 lps rem on hook, insert hook into st on motif, yo, draw through all rem lps.

Small Flowers
Make 6

Center Ring

Rnd 1: Ch 10, join to form a ring, ch 1, work 15 sc in ring, join.

Small Petals

Rnd 2: *Ch 10, turn, sl st in same st, ch 1, turn, [1 sc, 2 hdc, 3 dc, 2 tr, 3 dc, 2 hdc and 1 sc] in the ch-10 lp, sc in same st as lp was started. Sc in next 2 sc on Rnd 1 of center ring, sl st in next sc, rep from * 4 more times. After the 5 petals are completed, fasten off.

Assembly

Sew petals to motifs, with 3 petals to motifs and 2 petals to large flower petals. If desired, crochet together in same manner as Large Flowers were joined.

—Designed by Rosanne Kropp

The Things That Count

Not what we have, but what we use,
Not what we see, but what we choose;
These are the things that mar or bless
The sum of human happiness.

Not what we take, but what we give,
Not as we pray, but as we live;
These are the things that make for peace,
Both now and after time shall cease.

—Anonymous

Perfect Pineapples

*Create a collection of exquisite designs featuring a traditional favorite—
the pineapple. As your piece progresses round by round,
you'll experience sheer delight as each pineapple motif almost
magically appears! For those who have never crocheted a pineapple
doily, we've included a beginner pattern just for you, Easy Pineapple
Doily, on Page 77.*

Easy Pineapple Doily

Dainty Delight

Pineapple Circle

Pineapple Illusion

Radiant Star

Easy Pineapple Doily

*Beginners can learn the basics of crocheting pineapple lace
with this lovely, yet simple, doily worked in pretty shades of yellow.*

Experience Level

Beginner

Size

17" in diameter

Materials

• Crochet cotton size 10: 1 ball light yellow,
  1 ball shaded light yellows

• Size 5 steel crochet hook

Gauge

32 tr = 4" stretched and blocked

Pattern Note

Join rnds with a sl st unless otherwise stated.

Doily

*Note: Always count starting ch as first tr of
each rnd.*

Rnd 1: With shaded yellows, ch 8, join to
form a ring, ch 4, 1 tr in ring, *ch 2, 2 tr in ring,
rep from * 6 times, ending with ch 2, join in 4th
ch of beg ch-4. (8 ch-2 sps)

Rnd 2: Ch 4, tr in first tr, *ch 5, tr in each
of next 2 tr, rep from * around, ending with ch
5, join in 4th ch of beg ch-4. (8 ch-5 sps)

Rnd 3: Ch 4, tr in first tr, *[3 tr, ch 3, 3
tr] in next ch-5 sp, tr in each of next 2 tr,
rep from * around, ending with 3 tr in last

sp, join in 4th ch of beg ch-4.

Rnd 4: Ch 4, tr in each of next 2 tr, *ch 3,
[2 tr, ch 4, 2 tr] in next ch-3 sp, ch 3, sk next 2
tr, tr in each of next 4 tr, sk next 2 tr, rep from *
around, ending with tr in last tr, join in 4th ch
of beg ch-4.

Rnd 5: Ch 4, tr in each of next 2 tr, *ch 3,
[2 tr, ch 5, 2 tr] in next ch-4 sp, ch 3, tr in each
of next 4 tr, rep from * around, ending with tr
in last tr, join in 4th ch of beg ch-4.

Rnd 6: Ch 4, tr in each of next 2 tr, *[ch 3,
10 dtr] in next ch-5 sp, ch 3, tr in each of next
4 tr, rep from * around, ending with tr in last tr,
join in 4th ch of beg ch-4, fasten off shaded
yellows, attach light yellow.

Rnd 7: Ch 4, tr in each of next 2 tr, *ch 3,
[dtr in dtr, ch 1] 9 times, dtr in last dtr, ch 3, tr
in each of next 4 tr, rep from * around, ending
with tr in last tr, join in 4th ch of beg ch-4.

Rnd 8: Ch 4, tr in each of next 2 tr, ch 3,
*[sc, ch 4 in next ch-1 sp] 8 times, sc in next ch-
1 sp, ch 3, tr in each of next 4 tr, rep from *
around, ending with tr in last tr, join in 4th ch
of beg ch-4.

Rnd 9: Ch 4, tr in each of next 2 tr, ch 3,
*[sc, ch 4 in next ch-4 sp] 7 times, sc in next ch-
4 sp, ch 3, tr in each of next 4 tr, rep from *
around, ending with tr in last tr, join in 4th ch
of beg ch-4.

From this point, stop working all the way
around the doily. Each of the 8 "petals" is

Continued on Page 83

Dainty Delight

*This petite doily's pretty design and colored edging make it
the perfect place for setting a crystal vase filled with summer flowers!*

Getting Started

Experience Level
Beginner

Size
14½" in diameter

Materials
- Sport weight yarn: 2½ oz white, small amount pink
- Size D/3 crochet hook

Gauge
4 dc = ½"; 5 shell rnds = 2"

Pattern Note
Join rnds with a sl st unless otherwise stated.

Pattern Stitches
Beg shell: Sl st into ch-2 sp of shell, ch 3, dc, ch 2, 2 dc in same ch sp.

Shell: 2 dc, ch 2, 2 dc in same ch-2 sp.

Note: Both beg shell and shell will be referred to as shell. If rnd begins with a shell, work beg shell.

Doily
Rnd 1: With white, ch 4, join to form a ring, ch 3 (counts as first dc), 11 dc in ring, join. (12 dc)

Rnd 2: Working in back lps only, ch 3, dc in same st as beg ch-3, work 2 dc in each rem st around, join. (24 dc)

Rnd 3: Ch 3, dc, ch 2, 2 dc in same st, ch 1, sk 2 sts, [shell of 2 dc, ch 2, 2 dc in next st, ch 1, sk 2 sts] rep around, join. (8 shells)

Rnd 4: Sl st into ch-2 sp of shell, ch 3, [dc, ch 2, 2 dc] in same ch sp, ch 2, [shell of 2 dc, ch 2, 2 dc in ch-2 sp of shell, ch 2] rep around, join in 3rd ch of beg ch-3.

Rnd 5: [Shell in shell, ch 4] rep around, join in 3rd ch of beg ch-3.

Rnd 6: [Shell in shell, ch 6] rep around, join in 3rd ch of beg ch-3.

Rnd 7: [Shell in shell, ch 8] rep around, join in 3rd ch of beg ch-3.

Rnd 8: Sl st into ch-2 sp of shell, ch 3, 7 dc in ch-2 sp of shell, ch 8, [8 dc in next ch-2 sp of shell, ch 8] rep around, join in 3rd ch of beg ch-3.

Rnd 9: Ch 4 (counts as first dc, ch 1), dc in next dc, [ch 1, dc in next dc] 6 times, ch 6, *dc in next dc, [ch 1, dc in next dc] 7 times, ch 6, rep from * around, join in 3rd ch of beg ch-4.

Rnd 10: Ch 3 (counts as first dc), [dc in ch-1 sp, dc in next dc] 7 times, 5 sc over ch-6 sp, *dc in next dc, [dc in ch-1 sp, dc in next dc] 7 times, 5 sc over ch-6 sp, rep from * around, join.

Rnd 11: Ch 1, sc in same st, [ch 3, sk 1 dc, sc in next dc] 7 times, ch 1, sk 2 sc, shell of [2 dc, ch 2, 2 dc] in next sc, ch 1, *sc in next dc, [ch 3, sk 1 dc, sc in next dc] 7 times, ch 1, sk 2 sc, shell of [2 dc, ch 2, 2 dc] in next sc, ch 1, rep from * around, join in first sc.

Rnd 12: Ch 1, sc in ch-3 lp, [ch 3, sc in next ch-3 lp] 6 times, ch 1, 2 dc, ch 2, 2 dc, ch 2, 2 dc in next ch-2 sp of shell, ch 1, *sc in next ch-3 lp, [ch 3, sc in next ch-3 lp] 6 times, ch 1, 2 dc, ch 2, 2 dc, ch 2, 2 dc in next ch-2 sp of shell, ch 1, rep from * around, join.

Rnd 13: Ch 1, sc in ch-3 lp, [ch 3, sc in next ch-3 lp] 5 times, [ch 1, shell in next ch-2 sp] twice, ch 1, *sc in next ch-3 lp, [ch 3, sc in next ch-3 lp] 5 times, [ch 1, shell in next ch-2 sp] twice, ch 1, rep from * around, join in first sc.

Rnd 14: Ch 1, sc in ch-3 lp, [ch 3, sc in next ch-3 lp] 4 times, ch 1, shell in shell, shell in ch-1 sp, shell in shell, ch 1, *sc in next ch-3 lp, [ch 3, sc in next ch-3 lp] 4 times, ch 1, shell in shell, shell in ch-1 sp, shell in shell, ch 1, rep from * around, join in first sc.

Rnd 15: Ch 1, sc in ch-3 lp, [ch 3, sc in next ch-3 lp] 3 times, [ch 2, shell in shell] 3 times, ch 2, *sc in next ch-3 lp, [ch 3, sc in next ch-3 lp] 3 times, [ch 2, shell in shell] 3 times, ch 2, rep from * around, join in first sc.

Rnd 16: Ch 1, sc in ch-3 lp, [ch 3, sc in next ch-3 lp] twice, ch 2, shell in shell, ch 3, shell of [2 dc, ch 4, 2 dc] in next shell, ch 3, shell in shell, ch 2, *sc in next ch-3 lp, [ch 3, sc in next ch-3 lp] twice, ch 2, shell in shell, ch 3, shell of [2 dc, ch 4, 2 dc] in next shell, ch 3, shell in shell, ch 2, rep from * around, join in first sc.

Rnd 17: Ch 1, *sc in ch-3 lp, ch 3, sc in next ch-3 lp, ch 2, shell in shell, ch 3, 12 dc in ch-4 sp of shell, ch 3, shell in shell, ch 2, rep from * around, join in first sc.

Rnd 18: Ch 1, sl st into rem ch-3 lp, ch 5 (counts as first dc, ch 2), shell in shell, ch 3, dc in next dc of 12-dc group, [ch 1, dc in next dc] 11 times, ch 3, shell in shell, ch 2, *1 dc in rem ch-3 lp of pineapple, ch 2, shell in shell, ch 3, dc in next dc of 12-dc group, [ch 1, dc in next dc] 11 times, ch 3, shell in shell, ch 2, rep from * around, join in 3rd ch of beg ch-5, draw up a lp of pink, fasten off white.

Rnd 19: Ch 1, *sc in dc, 2 sc in ch-2 sp, sc in each of next 2 dc, 2 sc in ch-2 sp, sc in each of next 2 dc, 2 sc over ch-3 sp, sc in next dc, [sc in ch-1 sp, sc in next dc] 11 times, 2 sc over ch-3 sp, sc in next 2 dc, 2 sc in ch-2 sp, sc in each of next 2 dc, 2 sc over next ch-2 sp, rep from * around, join in first sc.

Rnd 20: Ch 3, 2 dc in same st, sk 1 st, sl st in next st, sk 1 st, *3 dc in next st, sk 1 st, sl st in next st, sk 1 st, rep from * around, join, fasten off.

Center Petal

Rnd 1: Attach pink in rem free lp of Rnd 1, ch 3, 2 dc in same st, sl st in next st, [3 dc in next st, sl st in next st] rep around, join, fasten off.

—Designed by Jocelyn Sass

Easy Pineapple Doily

Continued from Page 79

completed separately before beginning the next. Rep instructions below for each petal.

Petal

Row 1: Sl st into first tr on previous rnd, ch 4, tr in next tr, ch 3, [sc, ch 4 in next ch-4 sp] 6 times, sc in next ch-4 sp, ch 3, tr in each of next 2 tr, turn.

Row 2: Ch 4, tr in first tr, ch 3, [sc, ch 4 in next ch-4 sp] 5 times, sc in last ch-4 sp, ch 3, tr in each of next 2 tr, turn.

Row 3: Ch 4, tr in first tr, ch 3, [sc, ch 4 in next ch-4 sp] 4 times, sc in last ch-4 sp, ch 3, tr in next tr, tr in top of turning ch, turn.

Row 4: Ch 4, tr in first tr, ch 3, [sc, ch 4 in next ch-4 sp] 3 times, sc in last ch-4 sp, ch 3, tr in next tr, tr in top of turning ch, turn.

Row 5: Ch 4, tr in first tr, ch 3, [sc, ch 4 in next ch-4 sp] twice, sc in last ch-4 sp, ch 3, tr in next tr, tr in top of turning ch, turn.

Row 6: Ch 4, tr in first tr, ch 3, sc, ch 4 in next ch-4 sp, sc in last ch-4 sp, ch 3, tr in each of next 2 tr, turn.

Row 7: Ch 4, tr in first tr, ch 3, sc in next ch-4 sp, ch 3, tr in next tr, tr in top of turning ch.

Row 8: Ch 8, sl st in last tr on previous row, fasten off.

Edging

Rnd 1: Working up side of first petal, attach maize with a sl st in side of first ch-4 of Row 1, ch 4, dc in same sp, working along side of petal, [ch 4, *dc in next sp, ch 4, dc in same sp] 7 times, working in tip of petal, ch 4, {dc, ch 1} 5 times, dc in same sp, working along other side of first petal, rep bet [] 7 times, ch 1, rep from * around, join to first sl st of rnd.

Rnd 2: Sl st in first sp, *ch 5, sl st in 3rd ch from hook (picot made), ch 2, sk next sp, sc in next sp, rep from * around, join to 3rd ch of beg ch-5, fasten off.

—Designed by Sylvia Landman

In Quietness Is Beauty

In quietness is beauty;

*The waveless pool reflects
More planets than the ocean,
The tranquil mind collects*

Immeasurable wisdom,

*And perfectly the rose
Portrays the art of silence,
The purpose of repose.*

Be clothed in contemplation;

*Let foolish striving cease,
Put on the shield of quiet
The diadem of peace,*

And through the lifted portal

*Of thought receive anew
The bounty of the Father,
The beautiful and true.*

—Vivian Yeiser Laramore

Pineapple Circle

*A center star of eight pineapples is surrounded
by still more pineapples on this enchanting doily.*

Getting Started

Experience Level
Intermediate

Size
Small Doily: 17" in diameter
Large Doily: 24" in diameter

Materials
Small Doily
- Crochet cotton size 30 (350 yds per ball): 2 balls ecru
- Size 12 steel crochet hook

Large Doily
- Crochet cotton size 10 (150 yds per ball): 5 balls ecru
- Size 7 steel crochet hook

Gauge
Work evenly and consistently throughout

Pattern Note
Join rnds with a sl st in the 3rd ch of beg ch-3 unless otherwise stated.

Doily

Rnd 1: Ch 8, join with sl st to form a ring, ch 3 (counts as beg dc), 19 dc in ring, join. (20 dc)

Rnd 2: Ch 7, sk 1 dc, dc in next dc, *ch 4, sk 1 dc, dc in next dc, rep from * around, ch 4, join in 3rd ch of beg ch-7. (10 ch-4 lps)

Rnd 3: Ch 3, *5 dc in next ch-4 lp, dc in next dc, rep from * around, ending with 5 dc in last lp, join. (60 dc)

Rnd 4: Ch 3, dc in each of next 13 dc, [2 dc in next dc, dc in each of next 14 dc] 3 times, 2 dc in last dc, join. (64 dc)

Rnd 5: Ch 3, 2 dc in base of ch-3, ch 3, 3 dc in same place, *ch 6, sk 7 dc, 5 tr in next dc, ch 6, sk 7 dc, [3 dc, ch 3, 3 dc] in next dc (shell), rep from * around, ending with ch 6, sk 7 dc, 5 tr in next dc, ch 6, join.

Rnd 6: Sl st to ch-3 shell sp, ch 3, [2 dc, ch 3, 3 dc] in same sp, *ch 6, 2 tr in each of next 5 tr, ch 6, shell in next shell sp, rep from * around, ending with ch 6, join.

Rnd 7: Sl st to ch-3 shell sp, ch 3, [2 dc, ch 3, 3 dc] in same sp, *ch 6, [2 tr in next tr, tr in next tr] twice, 2 tr in next tr, ch 1, 2 tr in next tr, [tr in next tr, 2 tr in next tr] twice, ch 6, shell in next shell, rep from * around, ending last rep with ch 6, join.

Rnd 8: Sl st to ch-3 shell sp, ch 3, [2 dc, ch 3, 3 dc] in same sp, *ch 5, sk 1 tr, [2 dc, ch 2, 2 dc] in next tr, ch 5, sk 6 tr, [3 dc, ch 3, 3 dc] in next ch-1 sp (shell), ch 5, sk 6 tr, [2 dc, ch 2, 2 dc] in next tr, ch 5, shell in next shell sp, rep from * around, ending last rep with ch 5, join.

Rnd 9: Sl st to ch-3 shell sp, ch 3, [2 dc, ch 3, 3 dc] in same sp, *ch 4, dc in ch-5 lp, dc in each of next 2 dc, ch 3, dc in each of next 2 dc, dc in next ch-5 lp, ch 4, shell in next shell, ch 4, dc in next ch-5 lp, dc in each of next 2 dc, ch 3, dc in each of next 2 dc, dc in next ch-5 lp, ch 4, shell in next shell, rep from * around, ending last rep with ch 4, join.

Rnd 10: Sl st to ch-3 shell sp, ch 3, [2 dc, ch 3, 3 dc] in same sp, *ch 4, dc in next ch-4 lp, dc in each of next 3 dc, [dc, ch 3, dc] in next ch-3 lp, dc in each of next 3 dc, dc in next ch-4 lp, ch 4, shell in next shell, rep from * around, ending last rep with ch 4, join.

Rnd 11: Sl st to ch-3 shell sp, ch 3, 2 dc in same sp, [ch 3, 3 dc] twice in same sp, *ch 2, dc in next ch-4 lp, dc in each of next 5 dc, [dc, ch 5, dc] in next ch-3 sp, dc in each of next 5 dc, dc in next ch-4 lp, ch 2, [3 dc, ch 3] twice in ch-3 shell sp, 3 dc in same sp, rep from * around, ending last rep with ch 2, join.

Rnd 12: Sl st to next ch-3 sp, ch 3, [2 dc, ch 3, 3 dc] in same sp, shell in next ch-3 sp, *ch 2, sk next dc, dc in each of next 5 dc, ch 2, 7 tr in 3rd ch of next ch-5 lp, ch 2, sk next dc, dc in each of next 5 dc, ch 2, [shell in next ch-3 sp] twice, rep from * around, ending last rep with ch 2, join.

Rnd 13: Sl st to next ch-3 shell sp, ch 3, [2 dc, ch 3, 3 dc] in same sp, *ch 1, shell in next shell, ch 2, sk next dc, dc in each of next 3 dc, ch 2, [tr in next tr, ch 1] 6 times, tr in next tr, ch 2, sk next dc, dc in each of next 3 dc, ch 2, shell in next shell, rep from * around, ending last rep with ch 2, join.

Rnd 14: Sl st to next ch-3 shell sp, ch 3, [2 dc, ch 3, 3 dc] in same sp, *ch 2, shell in next shell, ch 1, dc in each of next 2 dc, ch 2, sc in next ch-1 sp, [ch 3, sc in next ch-1 sp] 5 times, ch 2, sk next dc, dc in each of next 2 dc, ch 1, shell in next shell, rep from * around, ending last rep with ch 1, join.

Rnd 15: Sl st to next ch-3 shell sp, ch 3, [2 dc, ch 3, 3 dc] in same sp, *ch 4, shell in next shell, ch 1, dc in next dc, ch 3, sk next ch-2 sp, sc in first ch-3 lp of pineapple, [ch 3, sc in next

ch-3 lp] 4 times, ch 3, sk next dc, dc in next dc, ch 1, shell in next shell, rep from * around, ending last rep with ch 1, join.

Rnd 16: Sl st to next ch-3 shell sp, ch 3, [2 dc, ch 3, 3 dc] in same sp, *ch 5, sc in next ch-4 sp, ch 5, shell in next shell, ch 5, sk next 2 lps, sc in first ch-3 lp of pineapple, [ch 3, sc in next ch-3 lp] 3 times, ch 5, sk next 2 lps, shell in next shell, rep from * around, ending last rep with ch 5, join.

Rnd 17: Sl st to next ch-3 shell sp, ch 3, [2 dc, ch 3, 3 dc] in same sp, *ch 5, [sc in next ch-5 lp, ch 5] twice, shell in next shell, ch 5, sk next ch-5 lp, sc in first ch-3 lp of pineapple, [ch 3, sc in next ch-3 lp] twice, ch 5, shell in next shell, rep from * around, ending last rep with ch 5, join.

Rnd 18: Sl st to ch-3 shell sp, ch 3, [2 dc, ch 3, 3 dc] in same sp, *[ch 5, sc in next ch-5 lp] 3 times, ch 5, shell in next shell, ch 5, sc in first ch-3 lp of pineapple, ch 3, sc in next ch-3 lp, ch 5, shell in next shell, rep from * around, ending last rep with ch 5, join.

Rnd 19: Sl st to ch-3 shell sp, ch 3, [2 dc, ch 3, 3 dc] in same sp, *[ch 5, sc in next ch-5 lp] 4 times, ch 5, shell in next shell, ch 5, sc in rem ch-3 lp of pineapple, ch 5, shell in next shell, rep from * around, ending last rep with ch 5, join.

Rnd 20: Sl st to ch-3 shell sp, ch 3, [2 dc, ch 3, 3 dc] in same sp, *[ch 6, sc in next ch-5 lp] 5 times, ch 6, shell in next shell, ch 5, sc in sc at top of pineapple, ch 5, shell in next shell, rep from * around, ending last rep with ch 5, join.

Rnd 21: Sl st to ch-3 shell sp, ch 3, [2 dc, ch 3, 3 dc] in same sp, *[ch 7, sc in next ch-6 lp] 6 times, ch 7, [shell in next shell] twice, rep from * around, ending last rep with shell in last shell, join.

Rnd 22: Sl st to ch-3 shell sp, sc in same sp, *[ch 7, sc in next ch-7 lp] 7 times, [ch 7, sc in ch-3 sp of next shell] twice, rep from * around, ending last rep with ch 3, join with tr in first sc.

Rnd 23: *Ch 7, sc in next ch-7 lp, rep from * around, ending last rep with ch 3, join with a tr in tr.

Rnds 24–26: *Ch 8, sc in next lp, rep from * around, ending last rep with ch 4, join with tr in tr.

Rnd 27: *Ch 9, sc in next ch-8 lp, rep from * around, ending last rep with ch 4, join with dtr in tr.

Rnd 28: *Ch 9, sc in next ch-9 lp, rep from * around, ending last rep with ch 9, join with sl st in dtr.

Rnd 29: Sl st to 5th ch of next ch-9 lp, ch 3, [2 dc, ch 3, 3 dc] in same lp, *ch 5, sc in next ch-9 lp, ch 5, [2 dc, ch 2, 2 dc] in 5th ch of next ch-9 lp, ch 5, sc in next ch-9 lp, ch 5, [3 dc, ch 3, 3 dc] in 5th ch of next ch-9 lp (shell), rep from * around, ending last rep with ch 5, join.

Rnd 30: Sl st to ch-3 shell sp, ch 3, [2 dc, ch 3, 3 dc] in same sp, *ch 8, sk next ch-5 lp, dc in next ch-5 lp, dc in each of next 2 dc, ch 4, dc in each of next 2 dc, dc in next ch-5 lp, ch 8, shell in next shell, rep from * around, ending last rep with ch 8, join.

Rnd 31: Sl st to ch-3 shell sp, ch 3, [2 dc, ch 3, 3 dc] in same sp, *ch 8, dc in next ch-8 lp, dc in each of next 3 dc, [dc, ch 4, dc] in next ch-4 sp, dc in each of next 3 dc, dc in next ch-8 lp, ch 8, shell in next shell, rep from * around, ending last rep with ch 8, join.

Rnd 32: Sl st to ch-3 shell sp, ch 3, [2 dc, ch 3, 3 dc] in same sp, *ch 7, dc in next ch-8 lp, dc in each of next 5 dc, [dc, ch 4, dc] in next ch-4 sp, dc in each of next 5 dc, dc in next ch-8 lp, ch 7, shell in next shell, rep from * around, ending last rep with ch 7, join.

Rnd 33: Sl st to ch-3 shell sp, ch 3, 2 dc in same sp, [ch 3, 3 dc] twice in same sp, *ch 6, sk next dc, dc in each of next 5 dc, ch 2, 9 tr in next ch-4 sp, ch 2, sk next dc, dc in each of next 5 dc, ch 6, [3 dc, ch 3] twice in next ch-3 shell sp, 3 dc in same shell sp, rep from * around, ending last rep with ch 6, join.

Rnd 34: Sl st to ch-3 sp, ch 3, [2 dc, ch 3, 3 dc] in same sp, *shell in next ch-3 sp, ch 4, dc in each of next 4 dc, ch 2, [tr in next tr, ch 1] 8 times, tr in next tr, ch 2, sk next dc, dc in each of next 4 dc, ch 4, shell in next ch-3 sp, rep from * around, ending last rep with ch 4, join.

Rnd 35: Sl st to ch-3 shell sp, ch 3, [2 dc, ch 3, 3 dc] in same sp, *ch 3, shell in next shell, ch 2, dc in each of next 3 dc, ch 3, sc in first ch-1 sp, [ch 3, sc in next ch-1 sp] 7 times, ch 3, sk next dc, dc in each of next 3 dc, ch 2, shell in next shell, rep from * around, ending last rep with ch 2, join.

Rnd 36: Sl st to ch-3 shell sp, ch 3, [2 dc, ch 3, 3 dc] in same sp, *ch 3, sc in next ch-3 lp, ch 3, shell in next shell, ch 1, dc in each of next 2 dc, ch 3, sk next ch-3 lp, sc in first ch-3 lp of pineapple, [ch 3, sc in next ch-3 lp] 6 times, ch 3, sk next dc, dc in each of next 2 dc, ch 1, shell in next shell, rep from * around, ending last rep with ch 1, join.

Rnd 37: Sl st to ch-3 shell sp, ch 3, [2 dc, ch 3, 3 dc] in same sp, *[ch 3, sc in next ch-3 lp] twice, ch 3, shell in next shell, ch 1, sk next dc, dc in next dc, ch 2, sk next ch-3 lp, sc in first ch-3 lp, of pineapple, [ch 3, sc in next ch-3 lp] 5 times, ch 2, dc in next dc, ch 1, shell in next shell, rep from * around, ending last rep with ch 1, join.

Rnd 38: Sl st to ch-3 shell sp, ch 3, [2 dc, ch 3, 3 dc] in same sp, *[ch 4, sc in next ch-3 lp] 3 times, ch 4, shell in next shell, ch 3, sk

Continued on Page 91

Pineapple Illusion

This exquisite and airy doily will beautifully grace any end table in your home. Crochet it with ecru for a handsome antique look or with white for a soft, delicate aura.

Getting Started

Experience Level
Beginner

Size
21" in diameter

Materials
- Crochet cotton size 10: 325 yds ecru
- Size 7 steel crochet hook

Gauge
3 shell rnds = 1"; 3 dc = ¼"

Pattern Note
Join rnds with a sl st unless otherwise stated.

Pattern Stitches
Shell: 2 dc, ch 2 and 2 dc in indicated sp.

Beg shell: Sl st into indicated sp, ch 3 (counts as first dc), 1 dc, ch 2 and 2 dc in indicated sp.

Note: Both shell and beg shell will be referred to as a shell. If a rnd begins with a shell, simply work a beg shell.

Double shell: 2 dc, ch 2, 2 dc, ch 2 and 2 dc in same indicated sp.

Beg double shell: Sl st into indicated sp, ch 3 (counts as first dc), 1 dc, ch 2, 2 dc, ch 2 and 2 dc in same indicated sp.

Note: Both double shell and beg double shell will be referred to as a double shell. If a rnd begins with a double shell, simply work a beg double shell.

Doily
Rnd 1: Ch 8, join to form a ring, ch 3 (counts as first dc), 19 dc in ring, join in 3rd ch of beg ch-3. (20 dc)

Rnd 2: Ch 4 (counts as first dc, ch 1), [dc in next dc, ch 1] rep around, join in 3rd ch of beg ch-4.

Rnd 3: Ch 5 (counts as first dc, ch 2), [dc in next dc, ch 2] rep around, join in 3rd ch of beg ch-5.

Rnd 4: Sl st into ch-2 sp, ch 1, sc in same ch sp as beg ch-1, [ch 5, sc in next ch sp] rep around, ending with ch 2, join with dc in beg sc.

Rnd 5: Ch 1, sc in same ch sp, [ch 5, sc in next ch sp] rep around, ending with ch 2, join with dc in beg sc. (20 ch sps)

Rnd 6: Ch 3, dc, ch 2 and 2 dc in same ch sp, ch 3, sc in next ch sp, ch 3, [shell in next ch sp, ch 3, sc in next ch-sp, ch 3] rep around, join in 3rd ch of beg ch-3. (10 shells)

Rnd 7: [Shell in ch sp of shell, ch 6] rep around, join in 3rd ch of beg ch-3.

Rnd 8: [Shell in shell, ch 4, sc in ch-6 sp, ch 4] rep around, join in 3rd ch of beg ch-3.

Rnd 9: [Shell in shell, ch 10] rep around, join in 3rd ch of beg ch-3.

Rnd 10: [Shell in shell, ch 6, sc in ch-10 sp, ch 6] rep around, join in 3rd ch of beg ch-3.

Rnd 11: *Shell in shell, [ch 4, sc in next ch-6 sp] twice, ch 4, rep from * around, join in 3rd ch of beg ch-3.

Rnd 12: [Shell in shell, ch 3, sc in next ch-4 sp, ch 3, 7 dc in next ch-4 sp, ch 3, sc in next ch-4 sp, ch 3] rep around, join.

Rnd 13: *Shell in shell, ch 3, dc in next dc of 7-dc group, [ch 1, dc in next dc] 6 times, ch 3, rep from * around, join.

Rnd 14: *Double shell in shell, ch 3, sk next ch-3 sp, [sc in next ch-1 sp, ch 3] 6 times, rep from * around, join.

Rnd 15: *Shell in ch-2 sp of double shell, shell in next ch-2 sp of double shell, ch 3, sk next ch-3 sp, [sc in next ch-3 sp, ch 3] 5 times, rep from * around, join.

Rnd 16: *Shell in shell, ch 2, shell in shell, ch 3, sk next ch-3 sp, [sc in next ch-3 sp, ch 3] 4 times, rep from * around, join.

Rnd 17: *Shell in shell, ch 3, shell in shell, ch 3, sk next ch-3 sp, [sc in next ch-3 sp, ch 3] 3 times, rep from * around, join.

Rnd 18: [Shell in shell, ch 3, sc in ch-3 sp, ch 3, shell in shell, ch 4, sk next ch-3 sp, sc in next ch-3 sp, ch 3, sc in next ch-3 sp, ch 4] rep around, join.

Rnd 19: *Shell in shell, [ch 3, sc in next ch-3 sp] twice, ch 3, shell in shell, ch 4, sc in next ch-3 sp, ch 4, rep from * around, join.

Rnd 20: [Shell in shell, ch 5, sk next ch-3 sp, shell in next ch-3 sp, ch 5, shell in shell, ch 5] rep around, join.

Rnd 21: [Shell in shell, ch 6] rep around, join.

Rnd 22: [Shell in shell, ch 3, sc in ch-6 sp, ch 3, 7 dc in ch-2 sp of shell, ch 3, sc in next ch-6 sp, ch 3, shell in shell, ch 3, sc in next ch-6 sp, ch 3] rep around, join.

Rnd 23: *Shell in shell, ch 6, dc in first dc of 7-dc group, [ch 1, dc in next dc] 6 times, ch 6, shell in shell, ch 5, rep from * around, join.

Rnd 24: *Shell in shell, ch 6, [sc in next ch-1 sp, ch 3] 5 times, sc in next ch-1 sp, ch 6, shell in shell, ch 3, sc in next ch-5 sp, ch 3, rep from * around, join.

Rnd 25: *Shell in shell, ch 6, [sc in next ch-3 sp, ch 3] 4 times, sc in next ch-3 sp, ch 6, shell in shell, ch 6, rep from * around, join.

Rnd 26: *Shell in shell, ch 6, [sc in next ch-3 sp, ch 3] 3 times, sc in next ch-3 sp, ch 6, shell in shell, ch 4, sc in next ch-6 sp, ch 4, rep from * around, join.

Rnd 27: *Shell in shell, ch 7, [sc in next ch-3 sp, ch 3] twice, sc in next ch-3 sp, ch 7, shell in shell, [ch 4, sc in next ch sp] twice, ch 4, rep from * around, join.

Rnd 28: *Shell in shell, ch 7, sc in next ch-3 sp, ch 3, sc in next ch-3 sp, ch 7, shell in shell, [ch 4, sc in next ch sp] 3 times, ch 4, rep from * around, join.

Rnd 29: *Double shell in shell, ch 7, sc in ch-3 sp, ch 7, double shell in shell, [ch 4, sc in next ch sp] 4 times, ch 4, rep from * around, join.

Rnd 30: Sl st into ch-2 sp of shell, ch 3, 3 dc in same ch sp as beg ch-3, ch 1, 4 dc in next ch-2 sp of shell, ch 5, 4 dc in next ch-2 sp of shell, ch 1, 4 dc in next ch-2 sp of shell, [ch 4, sc in next ch sp] 5 times, ch 4, *4 dc in next ch-2 sp of shell, ch 1, 4 dc in next ch-2 sp of shell, ch 5, 4 dc in next ch-2 sp of shell, ch 1, 4 dc in next ch-2 sp of shell, [ch 4, sc in next ch sp] 5 times, ch 4, rep from * around, join.

Rnd 31: Sl st into ch-1 sp between 4-dc groups, ch 3, 3 dc in same ch-1 sp as beg ch-3, ch 8, 4 dc in next ch-1 sp, [ch 5, sc in next ch sp] 6 times, ch 5, *4 dc in next ch-1 sp, ch 8, 4 dc in next ch-1 sp, [ch 5, sc in next ch sp] 6 times, ch 5, rep from * around, ending with ch 3, dc in 3rd ch of beg ch-3.

Rnd 32: *Ch 9, sc in next ch-8 sp, ch 9, [sc in next ch sp, ch 6] twice, ch 3, 3 tr in next ch sp, ch 3, [sc in next ch sp, ch 6] twice, sc in next ch sp, rep from * around, ending with ch 3, tr in beg ch of ch-9.

Rnd 33: [Ch 8, sc in next ch sp] 4 times, *ch 8, sc in center tr of 3-tr group, [ch 8, sc in next ch sp] 6 times, rep from * around, ending with ch 4, dtr in beg ch of ch-8.

Rnd 34: [Ch 9, sc in next ch sp] rep around, ending with ch 4, dtr in beg ch of ch-9.

Rnd 35: Ch 10, [sc in next ch sp, ch 10] rep around, join in beg ch, fasten off.

—Designed by Della Brenneise

Pineapple Circle
Continued from Page 87

next dc and next ch-2 lp, sc in first ch-3 lp of pineapple, [ch 3, sc in next ch-3 lp] 4 times, ch 3, shell in next shell, rep from * around, ending last rep with ch 3, join.

Rnd 39: Sl st to ch-3 shell sp, ch 3, [2 dc, ch 3, 3 dc] in same sp, *[ch 4, sc in next ch-4 lp] 4 times, ch 4, shell in next shell, ch 3, sk next ch-3 lp, sc in first ch-3 lp of pineapple, [ch 3, sc in next ch-3 lp] 3 times, ch 3, shell in next shell, rep from * around, ending last rep with ch 3, join.

Rnd 40: Sl st to ch-3 shell sp, ch 3, [2 dc, ch 3, 3 dc] in same sp, *[ch 4, sc in next ch-4 lp] 5 times, ch 4, shell in next shell, ch 3, sk next ch-3 lp, sc in first ch-3 lp of pineapple, [ch 3, sc in next ch-3 lp] twice, ch 3, shell in next shell, rep from * around, ending last rep with ch 3, join.

Rnd 41: Sl st to ch-3 shell sp, ch 3, [2 dc, ch 3, 3 dc] in same sp, *[ch 5, sc in next ch-4 lp] 6 times, ch 5, shell in next shell, ch 3, sc in ch-3 lp of pineapple, ch 3, sc in next ch-3 lp, ch 3, shell in next shell, rep from * around, ending last rep with ch 3, join.

Rnd 42: Sl st to ch-3 shell sp, ch 3, [2 dc, ch 3, 3 dc] in same sp, *[ch 5, sc in next ch-5 lp] 7 times, ch 5, shell in next shell, ch 3, sc in rem ch-3 lp of pineapple, ch 3, shell in next shell, rep from * around, ending last rep with ch 3, join.

Rnd 43: Sl st to ch-3 shell sp, ch 3, [2 dc, ch 3, 3 dc] in same sp, *[ch 5, sc in next ch-5 lp] 8 times, ch 5, [shell in next shell] twice, rep from * around, ending last rep with shell in last shell sp, join.

Rnd 44: Sl st to ch-3 shell sp, sc in same sp, *[ch 6, sc in next ch-5 lp] 4 times, ch 1, tr in 3rd ch of next ch-5 lp, [ch 4, sl st in top of tr (picot), tr in same place] 5 times, ch 1, [sc in next ch-5 lp, ch 6] 4 times, sc in ch-3 sp of next shell, ch 4, sc in last sc (picot), sc in ch-3 sp of next shell, rep from * around, ending last rep with ch 6, sc in last ch-3 shell sp, ch 4, sc in last sc made (picot), join with a sl st in first sc, fasten off. ❖

Radiant Star

Like the petals opening on a flower, the points of the star designs stretch outward, accented with perfectly formed pineapples.

Getting Started

Experience Level
Advanced

Size
16" in diameter

Materials
- Crochet cotton size 30: 400 yds white
- Size 12 steel crochet hook

Gauge
7 tr = ½"; 4 tr rnds = 1"

Pattern Notes

Most clusters in this doily consist of 3 tr, but some contain other larger or smaller numbers of tr; work as indicated within pattern.

Join rnds with a sl st unless otherwise stated.

Pattern Stitch

Cluster (cl): Retaining last lp of each tr on hook, work indicated number of tr, yo, draw through all lps on hook. For beg cl, replace first tr with ch 4.

Doily

Rnd 1: Ch 6, join to form a ring, ch 6 (counts as first tr, ch 2), [tr in ring, ch 2] 7 times, join in 4th ch of beg ch-6.

Rnd 2: Sl st into ch-2 sp, ch 4, 4 tr in same ch-2 sp, ch 3, [5 tr in next ch-2 sp, ch 3] rep around, join in 4th ch of beg ch-4.

Rnd 3: Ch 4, tr in same st as beg ch-4, tr in each of next 3 tr, 2 tr in next tr, ch 4, [2 tr in each of next tr, tr in next 3 tr, 2 tr in next tr, ch 4] rep around, join in 4th ch of beg ch-4.

Rnd 4: Ch 4, tr in each of next 6 tr, ch 3, tr in ch-4 lp, ch 3, [tr in each of next 7 tr, ch 3, tr in ch-4 sp, ch 3] rep around, join in 4th ch of beg ch-4.

Rnd 5: Beg cl over next 3 tr, tr in next tr, cl over next 3 tr, ch 5, [tr, ch 5 and tr] in next tr, ch 5, [cl over next 3 tr, tr in next tr, cl over next 3 tr, ch 5, {tr, ch 5 and tr} in next tr, ch 5] rep around, join in 4th ch of beg ch-4.

Rnd 6: Beg cl over next 3 tr, ch 5, tr in next tr, ch 3, [tr, ch 3 and tr] in next ch-5 lp, ch 3, tr in next tr, ch 5, [cl over next 3 tr, ch 5, tr in next tr, ch 3, [tr, ch 3 and tr] in next ch-5 lp, ch 3, tr in next tr, ch 5] rep around, join in 4th ch of beg ch-4.

Rnd 7: Ch 9 (counts as first tr, ch 5), tr in next tr, ch 3, 3 tr in next tr, ch 5, 3 tr in next tr, ch 3, tr in next tr, [ch 5, tr in top of cl, ch 5, tr in next tr, ch 3, 3 tr in next tr, ch 5, 3 tr in next tr, ch 3, tr in next tr] rep around, ending with ch 2, tr in 4th ch of beg ch-9.

Rnd 8: Ch 4, tr in next ch-5 lp, ch 3, tr in next tr, ch 3, tr in each of next 3 tr, ch 5, tr in ch-5 lp, ch 5, tr in each of next 3 tr, ch 3, tr in next tr, [ch 3, retaining last lp of each tr, tr in each of next 2 ch sps, yo, draw through all lps on hook, ch 3, tr in next tr, ch 3, tr in each of next 3 tr, ch 5, tr in ch-5 lp, ch 5, tr in each of next 3 tr, ch 3, tr in next tr] rep around, ending with ch 1, hdc in 4th ch of beg ch-4.

Rnd 9: Ch 4, tr in next ch-3 lp, ch 3, tr in next tr, ch 1, tr in each of next 3 tr, ch 5, [tr, ch 5 and tr] in next tr, ch 5, tr in each of next 3 tr, ch 1, tr in tr, [ch 3, retaining last lp of each tr, tr in each of next 2 ch-3 lps, yo, draw through all lps on hook, ch 3, tr in next tr, ch 1, tr in each of next 3 tr, ch 5, [tr, ch 5 and tr] in next tr, ch 5, tr in each of next 3 tr, ch 1, tr in tr] rep around, ending with ch 1, hdc in 4th ch of beg ch-4.

Rnd 10: Ch 4, tr in next ch-3 lp, ch 1, tr in next tr, ch 1, tr in each of next 3 tr, ch 5, tr in next tr, ch 3, [tr, ch 3 and tr] in next ch-5 lp, ch 3, tr in next tr, ch 5, tr in each of next 3 tr, ch 1, tr in next tr, ch 1, [retaining last lp of each tr, tr in each of next 2 ch-3 lps, yo, draw through all lps on hook, ch 1, tr in next tr, ch 1, tr in each of next 3 tr, ch 5, tr in next tr, ch 3, [tr, ch 3 and tr] in next ch-5 lp, ch 3, tr in next tr, ch 5, tr in each of next 3 tr, ch 1, tr in next tr, ch 1] rep around, join in 4th ch of beg ch-4.

Rnd 11: Ch 4, sk tr at base of ch-4 and tr in next tr, ch 1, tr in each of next 3 tr, ch 5, tr in next tr, ch 3, 3 tr in next tr, ch 5, 3 tr in next tr, ch 3, tr in next tr, ch 5, tr in each of next 3 tr, [ch 1, retaining last lp of each tr on hook, tr in next tr, top of tr cl and next tr, yo, draw through all lps on hook, ch 1, tr in each of next 3 tr, ch 5, tr in next tr, ch 3, 3 tr in next tr, ch 5, 3 tr in next tr, ch 3, tr in next tr, ch 5, tr in each of next 3 tr] rep around, ending with ch 1, tr in next tr, join in 4th ch of beg ch-4.

Rnd 12: Sl st into ch-1 sp, sl st in next tr, ch 4, tr in each of next 2 tr, ch 5, tr in next tr, ch 3, tr in each of next 3 tr, ch 5, tr in ch-5 lp, ch 5, tr in each of next 3 tr, ch 3, tr in next tr, ch 5, tr in each of next 3 tr, ch 1, [tr in each of next 3 tr, ch 5, tr in next tr, ch 3, tr in each of next 3 tr, ch

5, tr in ch-5 lp, ch 5, tr in each of next 3 tr, ch 3, tr in next tr, ch 5, tr in each of next 3 tr, ch 1] rep around, join in 4th ch of beg ch-4.

Rnd 13: Ch 4, cl over next 2 tr, ch 5, tr in next tr, ch 3, tr in each of next 3 tr, ch 5, [tr, ch 5 and tr] in next tr, ch 5, tr in each of next 3 tr, ch 3, tr in next tr, ch 5, cl over next 2 tr, tr in next tr, [tr in next tr, cl over next 2 tr, ch 5, tr in next tr, ch 3, tr in each of next 3 tr, ch 5, [tr, ch 5 and tr] in next tr, ch 5, tr in each of next 3 tr, ch 3, tr in next tr, ch 5, cl over next 2 tr, tr in next tr] rep around, join in 4th ch of beg ch-4.

Rnd 14: Ch 9, tr in next tr, ch 3, tr in each of next 3 tr, ch 7, sk next ch-5 lp, 9 tr in next ch-5 lp, ch 7, sk next ch-5 lp, tr in each of next 3 tr, ch 3, tr in next tr, ch 5, [work 4-tr cl over next 4 tr, ch 5, tr in next tr, ch 3, tr in each of next 3 tr, ch 7, sk next ch-5 lp, 9 tr in next ch-5 lp, ch 7, sk next ch-5 lp, tr in each of next 3 tr, ch 3, tr in next tr, ch 5] rep around, ending with 3-tr cl over next 3 tr, join in 4th ch of beg ch-9.

Rnd 15: Ch 9, *tr in next tr, ch 3, 2 tr in next tr, tr in next tr, 2 tr in next tr, ch 5, tr in next tr, [ch 1, tr in next tr] 8 times, ch 5, 2 tr in next tr, tr in next tr, 2 tr in next tr, ch 3, tr in next tr, ch 5, tr in top of cl, ch 5, rep from * around, join in 4th ch of beg ch-9.

Rnd 16: Ch 7, *tr in next tr, ch 3, tr in each of next 2 tr, [tr, ch 3 and tr] in next tr, tr in each of next 2 tr, ch 5, sc in next ch-1 sp, [ch 5, sc in next ch-1 sp] 7 times, ch 5, tr in each of next 2 tr, [tr, ch 3 and tr] in next tr, tr in each of next 2 tr, [ch 3, tr in next tr] twice, ch 3, rep from * around, ending with ch-3, join in 4th ch of beg ch-7.

Rnd 17: Ch 6, tr in next tr, *ch 2, tr in each of next 3 tr, ch 2, tr in ch-3 lp, ch 2, tr in each of next 3 tr, ch 5, sk next ch-5 lp, sc in next ch-5 lp, [ch 5, sc in next ch-5 lp] 6 times, ch 5, tr in each of next 3 tr, ch 2, tr in next ch-3 lp, ch

2, tr in each of next 3 tr, [ch 2, tr in next tr] 3 times, rep from * around, ending with ch 2, join in 4th ch of beg ch-6.

Rnd 18: Ch 5, tr in next tr, *ch 1, tr in each of next 3 tr, ch 5, tr in next tr, ch 5, tr in each of next 3 tr, ch 5, sk next ch-5 lp, sc in next ch-5 lp, [ch 5, sc in next ch-5 lp] 5 times, ch 5, tr in each of next 3 tr, ch 5, tr in next tr, ch 5, tr in each of next 3 tr, [ch 1, tr in next tr] 3 times, rep from * around, ending with ch 1, join in 4th ch of beg ch-5.

Rnd 19: Sl st across to first tr of 3-tr group, ch 4, tr in each of next 2 tr, *ch 3, tr in ch-5 lp, ch 3, tr in next tr, ch 3, tr in ch-5 lp, ch 3, tr in each of next 3 tr, ch 5, sk next ch-5 lp, sc in next ch-5 lp, [ch 5, sc in next ch-5 lp] 4 times, ch 5, tr in each of next 3 tr, ch 3, tr in ch-5 lp, ch 3, tr in next tr, ch 3, tr in ch-5 lp, ch 3, tr in each of next 3 tr, ch 1, cl over next 3 tr, ch 1, tr in each of next 3 tr, rep from * around, ending with ch 1, join in 4th ch of beg ch-4.

Rnd 20: Ch 4, tr in each of next 2 tr, [ch 3, tr in ch-3 lp] 4 times, ch 3, tr in each of next 3 tr, ch 5, sk ch-5 lp, sc in next ch-5 lp, [ch 5, sc in next ch-5 lp] 3 times, ch 5, tr in each of next 3 tr, [ch 3, tr in next ch-3 lp] 4 times, ch 3, tr in each of next 3 tr, sk top of cl, tr in each of next 3 tr, rep from * around, ending with tr in each of next 3 tr, sk top of cl, sl st to join in 4th ch of beg ch-4.

Rnd 21: Ch 4, cl over next 2 tr, *[ch 4, tr in ch-3 lp] 5 times, ch 4, tr in each of next 3 tr, ch 5, sk next ch-5 lp, sc in next ch-5 lp, [ch 5, sc in next ch-5 lp] twice, ch 5, tr in each of next 3 tr, [ch 4, tr in next ch-3 lp] 5 times, ch 4, cl over next 2 tr, tr in each of next 2 tr, cl over next 2 tr, rep from * around, ending with cl over 2 tr, tr in next tr, join in 4th ch of beg ch-4.

Rnd 22: Ch 4, *[ch 4, tr in next ch-4 lp] 6 times, ch 4, tr in each of next 3 tr, ch 5, sk next

ch-5 lp, sc in next ch-5 lp, ch 5, sc in next ch-5 lp, ch 5, tr in each of next 3 tr, [ch 4, tr in next ch-4 lp] 6 times, ch 4, cl over next 4 tr, rep from * around, ending with cl over next 3 tr, sl st to join in 4th ch of beg ch-4.

Rnd 23: Sl st in next 2 chs of ch-4 lp, ch 4, *[ch 4, tr in next ch-4 lp] 6 times, ch 4, tr in each of next 3 tr, ch 5, sk next ch-5 lp, sc in next ch-5 lp, ch 5, tr in each of next 3 tr, [ch 4, tr in next ch-4 lp] 6 times, ch 4, retaining last lp of each tr, tr in each of next 2 ch-4 lps, yo, draw through all lps on hook, rep from * around, ending with ch 4, tr in next ch-4 lp, join in 4th ch of beg ch-4.

Rnd 24: Sl st in next 2 chs of ch-4 lp, ch 4, *[ch 5, tr in next ch-4 lp] 6 times, ch 5, tr in each of next 3 tr, ch 4, tr in each of next 3 tr, [ch 5, tr in next ch-4 lp] 6 times, ch 5, retaining last lp of each tr on hook, tr in each of next 2 ch-4 lps, yo, draw through all lps on hook, rep from * around, ending with ch 5, tr in next ch-4 lp, join in 4th ch of beg ch-4.

Rnd 25: Sl st in 3 chs of next ch-5 lp, ch 4, *[ch 5, tr in next ch-5 lp] 6 times, ch 5, tr in each of next 6 tr, [ch 5, tr in next ch-5 lp] 6 times, ch 5, retaining last lp of each tr on hook, tr in each of next 2 ch-5 lps, yo and draw through all lps on hook, rep from * around, ending with ch 5, tr in next ch-5 lp, join in 4th ch of beg ch-4.

Rnd 26: Sl st in 3 chs of next ch-5 lp, ch 4, tr in same st as beg ch-4, ch 7, sl st in 4th ch from hook, ch 3, 2 tr in same st as last tr, [in the next ch-5 lp work 2 tr, ch 7, sl st in 4th ch from hook, ch 3, 2 tr] 5 times, *ch 7, cl over next 6 tr, ch 7, [in next ch-5 lp work 2 tr, ch 7, sl st in 4th ch from hook, ch 3, 2 tr] 12 times, rep from * around, ending with join in 4th ch of beg ch-4, fasten off.

—Designed by Cindy Neyer

A Touch of Color

Choose your favorite color as the accent in a pretty doily to place under an antique lamp or favorite family photograph. Pretty flowers, dainty hearts, waving wheat and abundant ruffles are included in this colorful chapter.

Golden Wheat

Ring of Roses

Ruffled Points

Peppermint Hearts

Blue Hearts

Golden Wheat

This unique doily will remind you of a field filled with golden waves of grain being gently swayed by a cool autumn breeze.

Getting Started

Experience Level
Intermediate

Size
10" in diameter

Materials
- Crochet cotton size 10 (225 yds per ball): 1 ball each cream and shaded yellow
- Size 7 steel crochet hook

Gauge
9 sts = 1"; 4 tr rnds = 1¾"

Pattern Note
Join rnds with a sl st unless otherwise stated.

Pattern Stitch
Tr cluster (tr cl): Retaining last lp of each tr on hook, tr in each of next 3 tr, yo, draw through all 4 lps on hook.

Doily

Rnd 1: With cream, ch 6, join to form a ring, ch 7, sc in ring, [ch 6, sc in ring] 8 times, ch 3, tr in first ch of beg ch-7. (10 ch lps)

Rnd 2: [Ch 5, sc in next ch lp] 9 times, ch 2, tr in tr to join.

Rnd 3: [Ch 5, sc in next ch lp] rep around, sl st in tr to join.

Rnd 4: Sl st into next ch lp, ch 6 (counts as first dc, ch 3), dc in same ch lp, ch 3, [dc, ch 3 and dc in next ch lp, ch 3] rep around, join in 3rd ch of beg ch-6. (20 ch-3 sps)

Rnd 5: Sl st into next ch lp, ch 7 (counts as first dc, ch 4), [dc in next ch-3 lp, ch 4] rep around, join in 3rd ch of beg ch-7.

Rnd 6: Ch 1, sc in same dc as beg ch-1, ch 2, 3 tr, ch 1, tr, ch 1 and 3 tr in next dc, ch 2, [sc in next dc, ch 2, {3 tr, ch 1, tr, ch 1 and 3 tr} in next dc, ch 2] rep around, join in beg sc.

Rnd 7: Ch 4 (counts as first tr), tr cl over next 3 tr, ch 2, 3 tr, ch 1, 1 tr, ch 1 and 3 tr in next tr, ch 2, tr cl over next 3 tr, [tr in next sc, tr cl over next 3 tr, ch 2, 3 tr, ch 1, tr, ch 1 and 3 tr in next tr, ch 2, tr cl over next 3 tr] rep around, join in 4th ch of beg ch-4.

Rnd 8: Ch 5 (counts as first tr, ch 1), sk next cl, [tr cl over next 3 tr, ch 2, 3 tr, ch 1, tr, ch 1 and 3 tr in next tr, ch 2, tr cl over next 3 tr, ch 1, sk next cl, tr in next tr, ch 1, sk next cl] rep around, ending with join in 4th ch of beg ch-5.

Rnd 9: Ch 4, tr in same tr, [ch 2, sk next cl, tr cl over next 3 tr, ch 2, 3 tr, ch 1, tr, ch 1 and 3 tr in next tr, ch 3, tr cl over next 3 tr, ch 2, sk next cl, 2 tr in next tr] rep around, join in 4th ch of beg ch-4.

Rnd 10: Ch 7 (counts as first tr, ch 3), [tr in next tr, ch 4, sk next cl, tr cl over next 3 tr, ch 3, 3 tr in next tr, ch 3, tr cl over next 3 tr, ch 4, sk next cl, tr in next tr, ch 3] rep around, join in 4th ch of beg ch-7.

Rnd 11: Sl st into ch-3 sp, ch 5 (counts as

Continued on Page 103

Ring of Roses

*Reminiscent of flower garlands woven and worn by young girls, this pretty
doily features a wreath of vibrant flowers circling the doily's center.*

Getting Started

Experience Level
Advanced

Size
21" in diameter

Materials
- Crochet cotton size 10* (50 grams per ball): 2 balls ecru, 1 ball burgundy #818
- Size 7 steel crochet hook

Sample project was completed with DMC Cebelia.

Gauge
5 dc = ½"; flower motif = 2" across

Pattern Notes
The center portion of this doily is worked after completing the edge wreath of flowers.

Join rnds with a sl st unless otherwise stated.

Pattern Stitch
4-dc-cluster (4-dc cl): Keep last lp of each dc on hook, dc in 8th and 9th picot of any flower, dc in first and 2nd picot of next flower, thread over and draw through all 5 lps on hook.

Flower Motifs

First Flower Motif
Rnd 1: With burgundy, ch 8, join to form a ring, ch 7, [dc in ring, ch 3] 7 times, join in 4th ch of beg ch-7. (8 ch-3 sps)

Rnd 2: *Sc in next ch-3 sp, [hdc, dc, tr, dc, hdc, sc] in same sp (petal), rep from * around, join in first sc.

Rnd 3: [Ch 5, sl st between next 2 petals] 7 times, ch 5, join in first sl st. (8 ch-5 sps)

Rnd 4: *[Sc, hdc, dc, tr, dtr, tr, dc, hdc, sc] in next ch-5 sp, rep from * around, join in first sc, fasten off.

Rnd 5: Attach ecru in dtr of any petal, *ch 5, sl st in next dc of same petal, ch 5, sl st in dc of next petal, ch 5, sl st in dtr of same petal, rep from * around, ch 5, join in first sl st. (24 ch-5 lps)

Rnd 6: Sl st to center of next ch-5 lp, sc in same lp, *ch 6, sc in next lp, rep from * around, ending with ch 6, join in first sc.

Rnd 7: Sl st to center of next ch-6 lp, sc in same lp, *ch 5, sl st in 3rd ch from hook (picot), ch 2, sc in next ch-6 lp, rep from * around, ending last rep with ch 2, join in first sc, fasten off. (24 picot lps)

Second Flower Motif
Rnds 1–6: Rep Rnds 1–6 of First Flower Motif.

Rnd 7: Sl st to center of next ch-6 lp, sc in same lp, ch 3, join in picot of any lp of first flower (to join: drop lp from hook, insert hook in picot, pick up lp and pull through), [ch 3, sc in next ch-6 lp of Second Flower, ch 3, join in next picot of next lp of First Flower] twice, ch 3, sc in next ch-6 lp of Second Flower, [ch 5, sl st in 3rd ch from hook (picot), ch 2, sc in next lp of same motif] 21 times, ending last rep with sc in picot already worked in, fasten off.

Joining Third Flower Motif

With ecru, sl st to center of next ch-6 lp, sc in same lp, ch 3, join to 10th picot of Second Flower, *[ch 3, sc in next lp of Third Flower, ch 3, join in next picot of next lp of Second Flower] twice, ch 3, sc in next lp of Third Flower, [ch 2, picot, ch 2, sc in next lp] 21 times, ending last rep with sc in picot already worked in, fasten off. This leaves 9 picot lps between each flower on each side free.

Join 15 more flower motifs in the same way, joining last flower to First Flower. (18 flowers in wreath)

Doily Center

Rnds 1–6: Work Rnds 1–6 of First Flower Motif.

Rnd 7: Rep Rnd 6.

Rnd 8: Sl st into next ch-6 lp, ch 3, [dc, ch 1, 2 dc] in same lp, *[2 dc, ch 1, 2 dc] in next lp (shell), rep from * around, join in 3rd ch of beg ch-3.

Rnd 9: Sl st into ch-1 sp, ch 3, dc in same sp, *ch 5, 2 dc in next ch-1 sp, rep from * around, ending with ch 5, join in 3rd ch of beg ch-3.

Rnd 10: Sl st between ch-3 and next dc, ch 6, *[dc, ch 3, dc] in next ch-5 lp, ch 3, dc between next 2 dc, ch 3, rep from * around, ending with ch 3, join in 3rd ch of beg ch-6.

Rnd 11: *Sc in next ch-3 lp, [ch 5, sl st in 3rd ch from hook (picot)] twice, ch 2, sk next ch-3 lp, rep from * around, join in first sc.

Rnd 12: Sl st to center of next lp between picots, sc in lp, *[ch 2, picot] twice, ch 2, sc in next lp between picots, rep from * around, ending last rep with ch 2, join in first sc.

Rnd 13: Sl st to center of next lp between picots, sc in lp, *[ch 3, picot] twice, ch 3, sc in center of next lp between picots, rep from * around, ending with ch 3, join in first sc.

Rnd 14: Sl st to center of next lp between picots, ch 3, 2 dc in same place, *ch 6, 3 dc in center of next lp between picots, rep from * around, ending with ch 6, join in 3rd ch of beg ch-3.

Rnd 15: Sl st in next dc, ch 6, *dc, ch 2, dc in next ch-6 lp, ch 3, sk next dc, dc in next dc, ch 3, rep from * around, ending last rep with ch 3, join in 3rd ch of beg ch-6.

Rnd 16: Sl st in ch-3 lp, ch 6, *3 dc in next ch-2 lp, [ch 3, dc in next ch-3 lp] twice, ch 3, sk next ch-2 lp, [dc in next ch-3 lp, ch 3] twice, rep from * around, ending with ch 3, join in 3rd ch of beg ch-6.

Rnd 17: Sl st in next ch-3 lp, ch 3, dc in same lp, *dc in each of next 3 dc, 2 dc in next ch-3 lp, [ch 3, dc in next ch-3 lp] 3 times, ch 3, 2 dc in next ch-3 lp, rep from * around, ending with ch 3, join in 3rd ch of beg ch-3.

Rnd 18: Ch 3, dc in each of next 6 dc, *2 dc in next ch-3 lp, [ch 3, dc in next ch-3 lp] twice, ch 3, 2 dc in next ch-3 lp, dc in each of next 7 dc, rep from * around, ending last rep with 2 dc in last ch-3 lp, join in 3rd ch of beg ch-3.

Rnd 19: Ch 3, dc in each of next 8 dc, *2 dc in next ch-3 lp, ch 2, dc in next ch-3 lp, ch 2, 2 dc in next ch-3 lp, dc in each of next 11 dc, rep from * around, ending with 2 dc in last ch-3 lp, join in 3rd ch of beg ch-3.

Rnd 20: Ch 3, dc in each of next 10 dc, *2 dc in next ch-2 lp, ch 2, 2 dc in next ch-2 lp, dc in each of next 15 dc, rep from * around, ending last rep with dc in last 2 dc, join in 3rd ch of beg ch-3.

Rnd 21: Ch 3, dc in each of next 11 dc, *ch 2, sk next dc, dc in next ch-2 lp, ch 2, sk next dc, dc in each of next 17 dc, rep from * around, ending last rep with dc in each of last 5 dc, join in 3rd ch of beg ch-3.

Rnd 22: Ch 3, dc in each of next 10 dc, *ch 2, sk next dc, [dc in next ch-2 lp, ch 2] twice, sk next dc, dc in each of next 15 dc, rep from * around, ending last rep with dc in each of last 4 dc, join in 3rd ch of beg ch-3.

Rnd 23: Ch 3, dc in each of next 9 dc, *ch 2, sk next dc, [dc in next ch-2 lp, ch 2] 3 times, sk next dc, dc in each of next 13 dc, rep from * around, ending last rep with dc in each of last 3 dc, join in 3rd ch of beg ch-3.

Rnd 24: Ch 3, dc in each of next 8 dc, *ch 2, sk next dc, [dc in next ch-2 lp, ch 2] 4 times, sk next dc, dc in each of next 11 dc, rep from * around, ending last rep with dc in each of last 2 dc, join in 3rd ch of beg ch-3.

Rnd 25: Ch 3, dc in each of next 7 dc, *ch 2, sk next dc, [dc in next ch-2 lp, ch 2] 5 times, sk next dc, dc in each of next 9 dc, rep from * around, ending last rep with dc in last dc, join in 3rd ch of beg ch-3.

Rnd 26: Ch 3, dc in each of next 6 dc, *ch 2, sk next dc, [dc in next ch-2 lp, ch 2] 6 times, sk next dc, dc in each of next 7 dc, rep from * around, ending last rep with ch 2, join in 3rd ch of beg ch-3.

Rnd 27: Sl st in next dc, ch 3, dc in each of next 4 dc, *ch 2, sk next dc, [dc in next ch-2 lp, ch 2] 7 times, sk next dc, dc in each of next 5 dc, rep from * around, ending last rep with ch 2, join in 3rd ch of beg ch-3.

Rnd 28: Sl st in next dc, ch 3, dc in each of next 2 dc, *ch 2, sk next dc, [dc in next ch-2 lp, ch 2] 8 times, sk next dc, dc in each of next 3 dc, rep from * around, ending last rep with ch 2, join in 3rd ch of beg ch-3.

Rnd 29: Sl st to next dc, ch 6, *dc in next ch-2 lp, [ch 3, dc in next ch-2 lp] 8 times, ch 3, sk next dc, dc in next dc, ch 3, rep from * around, ending last rep with ch 3, join in 3rd ch of beg ch-6.

Rnd 30: *Sc in next ch-3 lp, [ch 5, sl st in 3rd ch from hook (picot)] twice, ch 2, sk next ch-3 lp, rep from * around, ending last rep with ch 2, join in first sc.

Rnd 31: Sl st to center of next lp between picots, sc in lp, *[ch 2, picot] twice, ch 2, sc in center of next lp between picots, rep from * around, ending with ch 2, join in first sc, *do not cut thread.*

Join Doily to Flower Wreath

Sl st to center of next lp between picots, *ch 3, 4-dc cl over 8th and 9th picots of any flower in outside wreath and first and 2nd picots of next flower, [ch 3, join in next picot of same flower (see Rnd 7 of Flower Motif), ch 3, join in center between picots of next lp of doily] 5 times, rep from * around, ending last rep with ch 3, join in sl st, fasten off. ❖

Golden Wheat

Continued from Page 99

first tr, ch 1), [tr in same lp, ch 1] 6 times, *sc in next ch lp, ch 6, sk next cl, retaining last lp of each dc on hook, dc in each of next 3 tr, yo, draw through all 4 lps on hook, ch 6, sk next cl, sc in next ch lp, ch 1, [tr in next ch-3 sp, ch 1] 7 times, rep from * around, join, fasten off.

Rnd 12: Attach shaded yellow cotton in ch-6 lp before any 3-dc cl of Rnd 11, ch 1, [sc in ch-6 lp, ch 8, sc in next ch-6 lp, work 2 dc in each of next 8 ch-1 sps] rep around, join in beg sc.

Rnd 13: Sl st into 3rd ch of ch-8 lp, ch 1, *3 sc in ch-8 lp, ch 3, dc in top of last sc made, [retaining last lp of each tr on hook, tr in each of next 2 dc, yo, draw through all 3 lps on hook, ch 3, dc in top of 2-tr cl] 8 times, rep from * around, join, fasten off.

—Designed by Rosanne Kropp

Ruffled Points

*Crochet this sparkling winter doily for a pretty post-holiday season touch.
It looks just like an ice crystal that hasn't yet melted!*

Pattern Note
Join rnds with a sl st unless otherwise stated.

Pattern Stitch
Shell: 2 dc, ch 3, 2 dc in indicated st.

Doily

Rnd 1: With white, ch 6, join to form a ring, ch 3 (counts as first dc), 14 dc in ring, join in 3rd ch of beg ch-3. (15 dc)

Rnd 2: Ch 3, dc in same dc, work 2 dc in each rem dc around, join in 3rd ch of beg ch-3. (30 dc)

Rnd 3: [Ch 5, sk 2 dc, sc in next dc] rep around, join in 3rd ch of beg ch-5. (10 ch-5 lps around)

Rnd 4: Sl st into next lp, ch 3, dc, ch 3, 2 dc in same lp, ch 2, [shell, in next lp, ch 2] rep around, join. (10 shells)

Rnd 5: Sl st into ch-3 sp, in same sp work ch 3, dc, ch 3, 2 dc, [ch 2, 2 dc in ch-2 sp between shells, ch 2, shell in ch-3 sp of shell] rep around, join.

Rnd 6: Sl st into ch-3 sp, ch 3, dc, ch 3, 2 dc in same sp, [ch 2, dc in next dc, ch 2, dc in next dc, ch 2, shell in next ch-3 sp of shell] rep around, join.

Rnd 7: Sl st into ch-3 sp of shell, ch 3, dc, ch 3, 2 dc in same ch-3 sp, [ch 3, shell in next ch-2 sp between dc sts, ch 3, shell in next ch-3 sp of shell] rep around, join. (20 shells)

Rnd 8: Sl st into ch-3 sp of shell, ch 3, dc, ch 3, 2 dc in same sp, [ch 2, 2 dc in next ch lp between shells, ch 2, shell in next ch-3 sp of shell] rep around, join.

Rnd 9: Sl st into ch-3 sp of shell, ch 3, dc, ch 3, 2 dc in same sp, [ch 2, dc in next 2 dc between shells, ch 2, shell in next shell] rep around, join.

Rnd 10: Sl st into ch-3 sp of shell, ch 3, dc, ch 3, 2 dc in same sp, [ch 3, dc in next 2 dc between shells, ch 3, shell in next shell] rep around, join, fasten off white.

Rnd 11: Attach iris blue in ch-3 sp of shell, ch 1, sc in same sp, ch 13, [sc in next ch-3 sp of shell, ch 13] rep around, join.

Note: *In Rnd 12, work the dc sts around the ch, not into each ch.*

Continued on Page 111

Peppermint Hearts

Whether you crochet it as a special Valentine's Day decoration or as a thoughtful gift for your sweetheart, this pretty doily is sure to win your heart!

Getting Started

Experience Level
Beginner

Size
17" in diameter

Materials
- Mercerized crochet cotton size 10 (150 yds per ball): 1 ball white, 2 balls red
- Size 7 steel crochet hook

Gauge
5 dc = ½"; 4 dc rnds= 1"

Pattern Notes
Beg each rnd with ch 3 (counts as first dc unless otherwise indicated).

End each rnd by joining with sl st in top of beg ch-3, unless otherwise indicated.

Doily

Rnd 1: With white, ch 7, join to form a ring, [2 dc, ch 3] 7 times in ring.

Rnd 2: Sl st into ch-3 lp, [2 dc in center ch of ch-3 lp, ch 5] rep around, join, fasten off.

Rnd 3: Attach red in center ch of any ch-5 lp, [5 dc in center ch of ch-5 lp, ch 5] rep around. (7 hearts started; 35 dc around)

Rnd 4: [2 dc in each of first 2 dc, dc in next dc, 2 dc in each of next 2 dc, ch 4] rep around. (9 dc between each ch lp)

Rnd 5: [2 dc in first dc, dc in next dc, 2 dc in next dc, dc in each of next 3 dc, 2 dc in next dc, dc in next dc, 2 dc in next dc, ch 3] rep around. (13 dc between each ch lp)

Rnd 6: [2 dc in first dc, dc in each of next 11 dc, 2 dc in last dc, ch 2] rep around.

Rnd 7: [2 dc in first dc, dc in each of next 13 dc, 2 dc in last dc, ch 1] rep around. (17 dc between each ch lp)

Rnd 8: [2 dc in first dc, dc in each of next 7 dc, ch 1, sk next dc, dc in each of next 7 dc, 2 dc in last dc, ch 1] rep around. (9 dc between each ch sp)

Rnd 9: [Dc in each of next 7 dc, dec 1 dc over next 2 dc, ch 3, dec 1 dc over next 2 dc, dc in each of next 7 dc, ch 3] rep around, to join this rnd, sk top of ch-3, join in top of next dc.

Rnd 10: Dec 1 dc over next 2 dc, dc in each of next 4 dc, dec 1 dc over next 2 dc, ch 5, [dec 1 dc over next 2 dc, dc in each of next 4 dc, dec 1 dc over next 2 dc, ch 5] rep around, sk top of ch-3, join in top of next dc.

Rnd 11: Dec 1 dc over next 2 dc, dc in each of next 2 dc, dec 1 dc over next 2 dc, ch 7, [dec 1 dc over next 2 dc, dc in each of next 2 dc, dec 1 dc over next 2 dc, ch 7] rep around, join, fasten off.

Rnd 12: Attach white in first dc of any heart, [2 dc in first dc, ch 3, sk 2 dc, 2 dc in next dc,

Continued on Page 111

Blue Hearts

You won't feel blue when you crochet this pretty doily! Ample hearts make up the doily's primary motif, accented by an exquisite edging.

Getting Started

Experience Level
Intermediate

Size
12" in diameter

Materials
- Crochet cotton size 10: 250 yds blue
- Size 7 steel crochet hook

Gauge
Rnds 1 and 2 = 1½"

Pattern Note

Join rnds with a sl st unless otherwise stated.

Doily

Rnd 1: Ch 10, join to form a ring, ch 3 (counts as first dc), 15 dc in ring, join in 3rd ch of beg ch-3. (16 dc)

Rnd 2: Ch 3, dc at base of ch, ch 1, [2 dc in next dc, ch 1] rep around, join in 3rd ch of beg ch-3. (32 dc)

Rnd 3: Ch 1, sc in same st as joining, *ch 5, sk 3 sts, sc in next st, ch 3, sk 1 st, sc in next st, rep from * around, ending ch 3, join in beg sc. (8 ch-5 sps and 8 ch-3 sps)

Rnd 4: Sl st into ch-5 sp, ch 3, 2 dc in same sp, *ch 3, sc in ch-3 sp, ch 3, 3 dc in ch-5 sp, rep from * around, ending ch 3, sc in ch-3 sp, ch 3, join in 3rd ch of beg ch-3.

Rnd 5: Ch 3, dc at base of ch, dc in next dc, 2 dc in next dc, *[ch 3, sc in ch-3 sp] twice, ch 3, 2 dc in next dc, dc in next dc, 2 dc in next dc, rep from * around, ending [ch 3, sc in ch-3 sp] twice, ch 3, join in 3rd ch of beg ch-3.

Rnd 6: Ch 3, dc in next dc, ch 2, dc in next dc, ch 2, dc in each of next 2 dc, *ch 5, sk ch-3 sp, sc in next ch-3 sp, ch 5, sk ch-3 sp, dc in each of next 2 dc, ch 2, dc in next dc, ch 2, dc in each of next 2 dc, rep from * around, ending ch 5, sk ch-3 sp, sc in next ch-3 sp, ch 5, join in 3rd ch of beg ch-3.

Rnd 7: Ch 3, dc in next dc, *ch 3, 5 dc in next dc, ch 3, dc in each of next 2 dc, [ch 3, sc in next ch-5 sp] twice, ch 3, dc in each of next 2 dc, rep from * around, ending ch 3, 5 dc in next dc, ch 3, dc in each of next 2 dc, [ch 3, sc in next ch-5 sp] twice, join in 3rd ch of beg ch-3.

Rnd 8: Ch 3, dc in next dc, *ch 3, 2 dc in each of next 2 dc, ch 1, dc in next dc, ch 1, 2 dc in each of next 2 dc, ch 3, dc in each of next 2 dc, ch 1, dc in each of next 2 dc, rep from * around, ending ch 3, 2 dc in each of next 2 dc, ch 1, dc in next dc, ch 1, 2 dc in each of next 2 dc, ch 3, dc in each of next 2 dc, ch 1, join in 3rd ch of beg ch-3.

Rnd 9: Ch 3, dc in next dc, *ch 3, 2 dc in next dc, dc in each of next 3 dc, ch 2, dc in next dc, ch 2, dc in each of next 3 dc, 2 dc in next dc, ch 3, dc in each of next 4 dc, rep from * around, ending last rep with dc in each of next 2 dc, join in 3rd ch of beg ch-3.

Rnd 10: Ch 3, dc in next dc, *ch 3, 2 dc in next dc, dc in each of next 4 dc, ch 3, sc in next dc, ch 3, dc in each of next 4 dc, 2 dc in next dc, ch 3, dc in each of next 2 dc, ch 1, dc in each of next 2 dc, rep from * around, ending last rep dc in each of next 2 dc, ch 1, join in 3rd ch of beg ch-3.

Rnd 11: Ch 3, dc in next dc, *ch 3, dc in each of next 6 dc, ch 3, sc in next sc, ch 3, dc in each of next 6 dc, ch 3, dc in each of next 2 dc, ch 2, dc in each of next 2 dc, rep from * around, ending last rep dc in each of next 2 dc, ch 2, join in 3rd ch of beg ch-3.

Rnd 12: Ch 3, dc in next dc, *ch 3, sk 1 dc, dc in each of next 4 dc, dc, ch 1 and dc in next dc, 2 dc, hdc and sc in ch-3 sp, sc in next sc, sc, hdc and 2 dc in ch-3 sp, dc, ch 1 and dc in next dc, dc in each of next 4 dc, [ch 3, dc in next 2 dc] twice, rep from * around, ending last rep ch 3, dc in each of next 2 dc, ch 3, join in 3rd ch of beg ch-3.

Rnd 13: Ch 3, dc in next dc, *ch 3, dc in next dc, ch 3, dc in ch-1 sp, ch 7, dc in next ch-1 sp, ch 3, sk 4 dc, dc in next dc, [ch 3, dc in each of next 2 dc] twice, rep from * around, ending last rep ch 3, dc in each of next 2 dc, ch 3, join in 3rd ch of beg ch-3.

Rnd 14: Ch 3, dc in next dc, *[ch 3, 2 dc in next dc] twice, ch 3, 2 dc in 4th ch of ch-7, [ch 3, 2 dc in next dc] twice, [ch 3, dc in each of next 2 dc] twice, rep from * around, ending last rep ch 3, dc in each of next 2 dc, ch 3, join in 3rd ch of beg ch-3.

Rnd 15: Ch 3, dc in next dc, *[ch 3, dc in each of next 2 dc] 6 times, ch 4, dc in each of next 2 dc, rep from * around, ending last rep [ch 3, dc in each of next 2 dc] 6 times, ch 4, join in 3rd ch of beg ch-3.

Rnd 16: Ch 3, dc in next dc, *[ch 3, dc in each of next 2 dc] 6 times, ch 5, dc in each of next 2 dc, rep from * around, ending last rep [ch 3, dc in each of next 2 dc] 6 times, ch 5, join in 3rd ch of beg ch-3.

Rnd 17: Ch 3, dc in next dc, *[ch 3, dc in each of next 2 dc] 6 times, ch 7, dc in each of next 2 dc, rep from * around, ending last rep [ch 3, dc in each of next 2 dc] 6 times, ch 7, join in 3rd ch of beg ch-3, ch 3.

Rnd 18: Dc in next dc, *[ch 3, dc in each of next 2 dc] 6 times, 13 dc in ch-7 sp, dc in each of next 2 dc, rep from * around, end last rep 13 dc in ch-7 sp, join in 3rd ch of beg ch-3.

Rnd 19: Sl st to next st, ch 6, dc in each of next 2 dc, [ch 3, dc in each of next 2 dc] 4 times, *ch 3, dc in next dc, [ch 1, dc in next dc] 3 times, ch 1, sk 1 dc, [dc, ch 3, dc] in next dc, sk 1 dc, [ch 1, sk 1 dc, dc in next dc] 4 times, [ch 3, dc in each of next 2 dc] 5 times, rep from * around, ending last rep ch 3, dc in next dc, [ch 1, sk 1 dc, dc in next dc] 3 times, ch 1, sk 1 dc, [dc, ch 3, dc] in next dc, sk 1 dc, [ch 1, sk 1 dc, dc in next dc] 3 times, ch 1, join in 3rd ch of beg ch-6.

Rnd 20: *[Ch 5, sc in each of next 2 dc] 5 times, ch 5, sc in next dc, [ch 3, sc in next dc] 4 times, ch 5, sc in next dc, [ch 3, sc in next dc] 4 times, rep from * around, join in 5th ch of beg ch-5, fasten off.

—Designed by Ruth Shepherd

Ruffled Points

Continued from Page 105

Rnd 12: Sl st into ch sp, ch 3, work 12 dc in same ch lp, work 13 dc in each rem ch lp around, join, fasten off iris blue.

Rnd 13: Attach white in 7th dc of next group of dc sts, ch 1, sc in same st, [ch 15, sc in 7th dc of next group] rep around, join.

Note: *In Rnd 14, work sts into the specified chs.*

Rnd 14: Ch 6 (counts as first dc, ch 3), sk 1 ch, sc in next ch, ch 3, sk 1 ch, sc in next ch, ch 3, sc in next ch, ch 3, dc in next ch, ch 3, sk 2 chs, dc in next ch, ch 3, sc in next ch, ch 3, sk 1 ch, sc in next ch, ch 3, sk 1 ch, sc in next ch, ch 3, sk 1 ch, dc in next sc, [ch 3, sk 1 ch, sc in next ch, ch 3, sk 1 ch, sc in next ch, ch 3, sc in next ch, ch 3, dc in next ch, ch 3, sk 2 chs, dc in next ch, ch 3, sc in next ch, ch 3, sk 1 ch, sc in next ch, ch 3, sk 1 ch, sc in next ch,

ch 3, sk 1 ch, dc in next sc] rep around, ending with ch 3, join in 3rd ch of beg ch-6.

Rnd 15: *[Ch 3, sc in next lp] 4 times, ch 3, dc in next dc, ch 3, dc in next dc, [ch 3, sc in next lp] 4 times, ch 3, sc in next dc, rep from * around, ending with ch 1, dc in beg ch-3.

Rnd 16: [Ch 3, sc in next ch lp] 5 times, *[ch 3, dc in next dc] twice, [ch 3, sc in next lp] 10 times, rep from * around, ending with [ch 3, sc in next lp] 5 times, ch 1, dc in beg ch-3.

Rnds 17–22: Rep Rnd 16, having 1 extra ch lp in each group of chs on each rnd. At the end of Rnd 22, fasten off white.

Rnd 23: Attach iris blue in ch before a dc st, *ch 3, dc in next dc, 3 dc, ch 3, sc at base of ch-3 (picot), 3 dc in same sp, dc in next dc, [ch 3, sc in next ch lp] 17 times, rep from * around, join, fasten off.

—Designed by Mary Viers

Peppermint Hearts

Continued from Page 107

ch 3, 2 dc in center ch of ch-7 lp, ch 3] rep around. (84 dc sts around)

Rnds 13 & 14: Sl st into center ch of ch-3 lp, [2 dc in center ch of ch-3 lp, ch 3] rep around, join.

Rnds 15–18: Sl st into center ch of ch lp, [2 dc in center ch of ch lp, ch 5] rep around, fasten off at end of Rnd 18.

Rnd 19: Attach red in center ch of any ch-5 lp, [5 dc in center ch of ch lp, ch 5, in center ch of next ch lp work 1 sc, ch 3, sc in same ch lp, ch 5] rep around. (21 hearts started; 105 dc sts around)

Rnd 20: [2 dc in each of first 2 dc, dc in next dc, 2 dc in each of last 2 dc, ch 7] rep around. (9 dc between ch lps)

Rnd 21: [2 dc in first dc, dc in next dc, 2 dc in next dc, dc in each of next 3 dc, 2 dc in next dc, dc in next dc, 2 dc in next dc, ch 5] rep around. (13 dc between ch lps)

Rnd 22: [2 dc in first dc, dc in each of next 11 dc, 2 dc in last dc, ch 3] rep around. (15 dc between ch lps)

Rnds 23–29: Rep Rnds 7–13, fasten off at end of Rnd 29.

Note: *To make smaller matching doilies, work Rnds 1–13, then fasten off.*

—Designed by Zelda Snyder

Classic Elegance

Capture the elegance of the Victorian era with these breathtaking crocheted doilies. The beautiful elegance of each delicate doily, reminiscent of gentler times, will forever remain a lovely addition to your home decor.

Kaleidoscope Centerpiece

Fancy Fans

Classy Clusters

Wheat & Grape Doily

Wheels Within a Wheel

Kaleidoscope Centerpiece

Featured on our cover, this beautiful centerpiece will become a treasured heirloom. Crochet it for a special holiday dinner or family gathering.

Getting Started

Experience Level
Intermediate

Size
20" in diameter

Materials
- Crochet cotton size 10: 400 yds white
- Size 7 steel crochet hook

Gauge
8 dc and 3 dc rows = 1"

Pattern Note
Join rnds with a sl st unless otherwise stated.

Pattern Stitches
Beg shell: Sl st into ch-2 sp, ch 3, dc, ch 2 and 2 dc in same ch sp of sh.

Shell: 2 dc, ch 2 and 2 dc in ch sp of sh.

Doily

Rnd 1: Ch 10, join to form a ring, ch 1, 16 sc in ring, join in first st. (16 sc)

Rnd 2: [Ch 5, sk 1 sc, sc in next sc] 7 times, ch 2, join with a dc in first sc of Rnd 1.

Rnd 3: [Ch 6, sc in next ch-5 lp] 7 times, ch 3, join with a dc in beg ch-6.

Rnd 4: [Ch 6, sc in next ch-6 lp] 7 times, ch 6, join in beg ch-6.

Rnd 5: Sl st in next ch-6 sp, ch 3 (counts as first dc), 6 dc in same sp, [ch 1, 7 dc in next ch sp] 7 times, ch 1, join in beg ch-3.

Rnd 6: Sc in ch-1 sp just made, [ch 6, sc in top of 4th dc (center dc of 7-dc group), ch 6, sc in ch-1 sp] 7 times, ch 6, sc in top of 4th dc, ch 3, join with a tr in beg sc.

Rnd 7: [Ch 6, sc in next lp] 15 times, ch 3, join with a tr in beg ch-6.

Rnd 8: [Ch 7, sc in next lp] 15 times, ch 7, join with a sc in beg ch-7.

Rnd 9: Sl st in first 2 chs of next ch-7, sc, hdc, dc, hdc and sc in same sp, [ch 5, sc, hdc, dc, hdc and sc in next sp] 15 times, ch 3, join with a dc in first sc.

Rnd 10: [Ch 5, sc in dc, ch 5, sc in ch-5 sp] 15 times, ch 3, join with a dc in beg ch-5.

Rnds 11 & 12: [Ch 5, sc in next ch sp] rep around, ending with ch 3, join with a dc in beg ch-5.

Rnd 13: [Ch 6, sc in next ch sp] rep around, ending with ch 6, join with a sc in beg ch-6.

Rnd 14: Sl st in first 2 chs of next ch-6 sp, sc, hdc, dc, hdc and sc in same sp, [ch 5, sc in next sp, ch 5, in next ch sp work sc, hdc, dc, hdc and sc] 15 times, ending with ch 3, join with a dc in first sc of rnd.

Rnd 15: *Ch 5, sc in dc, [ch 5, sc in next ch-5 sp] twice, rep from * around, ending with ch 5, sc in dc, ch 5, sc in ch sp, ch 3, join with a dc in beg ch-5.

Rnd 16: [Ch 5, sc in next ch sp] rep around, ending with ch 3, join with a dc in beg ch-5.

Rnd 17: [Ch 6, sc in next ch sp] rep around, ending with ch 3, join with a tr in beg ch-6.

Rnd 18: [Ch 6, sc in next ch sp] rep around, ending with ch 6, join in beg ch-6.

Rnd 19: Sl st in next lp, ch 3, 4 dc in same lp, work 5 dc in each rem lp around, join in beg st. (240 dc)

Rnd 20: Ch 3, dc in each of next 9 dc, ch 1, [dc in each of next 10 dc, ch 1] rep around, join in beg ch-3.

Rnd 21: Sl st in next dc, ch 3, dc in each of next 7 dc, [ch 3, sc in ch-1 sp, ch 3, sk 1 dc, dc in each of next 8 dc] rep around, ending with ch 3, sc in ch-1 sp, ch 3, join in beg st.

Rnd 22: Sl st in next dc, ch 3, dc in each of next 5 dc, *[ch 2, sc in ch-3 sp] twice, ch 2, sk next dc, dc in each of next 6 dc, rep from * around, ending with [ch 2, sc in ch-3 sp] twice, ch 2, join in beg st.

***Note:** For ease in following pattern, fasten off thread and attach thread in the 2nd ch-2 lp (center lp) of any such grouping.*

Rnd 23: Ch 3, dc, ch 2 and 2 dc in ch-2 sp, ch 2, sc in next ch-2 sp, ch 2, *sk 1 dc, dc in each of next 4 dc, ch 2, sc in next ch-2 sp, ch 2, 2 dc, ch 2 and 2 dc (shell) in next sp, ch 2, sc in next ch-2 sp, ch 2, rep from * around, ending with sk 1 dc, dc in each of next 4 dc, ch 2, sc in ch-2 sp, ch 2, join in beg ch-3.

Rnd 24: Beg shell, *ch 2, sk next ch-2 sp, sc in next ch-2 sp, ch 2, sk 1 dc, dc in each of next 2 dc, ch 2, sc in ch-2 sp, ch 2, sk next ch-2 sp, shell over shell, rep from * around, ending with ch 2, sk ch-2 sp, sc in next ch-2 sp, ch 2, sk next dc, dc in each of next 2 dc, ch 2, sc in next ch-2 sp, ch 2, join in beg st.

Rnd 25: Beg shell, *ch 4, sk next ch-2 sp, sc in next ch-2 sp, sc in each of next 2 dc, sc in next ch-2 sp, ch 4, sk ch-2 sp, shell over shell, rep from * around, ending with ch 4, sk ch-2 sp, sc in next sp, sc in each of next 2 dc, sc in next sp, ch 4, sk ch-2 sp, join in beg st.

Rnd 26: Beg shell, *ch 4, sc in ch-4 sp, sc in each of next 4 sc, sc in ch-4 sp, ch 4, shell over shell, rep from * around, ending with ch 4, sc in ch-4 sp, sc in each of next 4 sc, sc in ch-4 sp, ch 4, join in beg st.

Rnd 27: Beg shell, *ch 4, sc in ch-4 sp, sc in each of next 6 sc, sc in ch-4 sp, ch 4, shell over shell, rep from * around, ending with ch 4, sc in ch-4 sp, sc in each of next 6 sc, sc in ch-4 sp, ch 4, join in beg st.

Rnd 28: Sl st into ch-2 sp of shell, ch 3, dc, ch 3, 2 dc in same ch sp, *ch 4, sc in ch-4 sp, sc in each of next 8 sc, sc in ch-4 sp, ch 4, 2 dc, ch 3, 2 dc in ch-2 sp of shell, rep from * around, ending with ch 4, sc in ch-4 sp, sc in each of next 8 sc, sc in ch-4 sp, ch 4, join in beg st.

Rnd 29: Sl st into ch-3 sp of shell, ch 3, dc, [ch 2, 2 dc] twice in same ch sp, *ch 5, sk ch-4 sp and next sc, sc in each of next 8 sc, ch 5, sk next sc and ch-4 sp, [2 dc, ch 2] twice and 2 dc in next ch-3 sp of shell, rep from * around, ending with ch 5, sk next ch-4 sp and 1 sc, sc in each of next 8 sc, sk next sc and ch-4 sp, ch 5, join in beg st.

Rnd 30: Beg shell, ch 1, shell in next ch-2 sp, *ch 6, sk ch-5 sp and next sc, sc in each of next 6 sc, ch 6, sk next sc and next ch-5 sp, shell in ch-2 sp of shell, ch 1, shell in next ch-2 sp of shell, rep from * around, ending with ch

6, sk 1 sc and ch-5 sp, sc in each of next 6 sc, sk next sc and next ch-5 sp, ch 5, join in beg st.

Rnd 31: Beg shell, ch 2, shell in next shell, *ch 7, sk ch-6 sp and next sc, sc in each of next 4 sc, ch 7, sk next sc and next ch-6 sp, shell in shell, ch 2, shell in shell, rep from * around, ending with ch 7, sk ch-6 sp and sk next sc, sc in each of next 4 sc, ch 7, sk next sc and next ch-6 sp, join in beg st.

Rnd 32: Beg shell, *ch 3, sc in ch-2 sp, ch 3, shell over shell, ch 7, sk next sc, dc in each of next 2 sc, ch 7, sk next sc, shell over shell, rep from * around, ending with ch 3, sc in ch-2 sp, ch 3, shell over shell, ch 7, sk 1 sc, dc in each of next 2 sc, ch 7, join in beg st.

Rnd 33: Beg shell, *[ch 3, sc in next ch sp] twice, ch 3, shell over shell, ch 2, shell over shell, rep from * around, ending with [ch 3, sc in next ch sp] twice, ch 3, shell

over shell, ch 2, join in beg st.

Rnd 34: Sl st into ch-2 sp of shell, ch 1, sc in same ch-2 sp of shell, *[ch 4, sc in next ch-3 sp] 3 times, ch 4, sc in next ch-2 sp of shell, ch 4, sk ch-2 sp between shells, sc in ch-2 sp of shell, rep from * around, ending with ch 2, join with a dc in beg sc.

Rnds 35–38: [Ch 5, sc in next ch lp] rep around, ending with ch 3, join with a dc in beg ch-5.

Rnd 39: Ch 5, sc in next ch-5 sp, *ch 2, in next ch sp work 2 dc, ch 5, sl st in 5th ch for picot, 2 dc in same ch sp, ch 2, sc in next ch sp, [ch 5, sc in next ch sp] 3 times, rep from * around, ending with ch 2, in next ch sp work 2 dc, ch 5, sl st in 5th ch from hook and 2 dc in same ch sp, ch 2, sc in next ch sp, ch 5, sc in next ch sp, ch 5, join in beg ch-5, fasten off. ❖

A Rose of Joy

As when one wears a fragrant rose
Close to the heart, a rose most fair,
And while the day's life onward flows,
Forgets that it is fastened there;

And wonders what delicious charm
Dwells in the air about, and whence
Come the rich wafts of perfume warm,
Subtly saluting soul and sense;

And then, remembering what it is,
Bends smiling eyes the flower above,
Adores its beauty and its bliss
And looks on it with grateful love—

Even so I wear, O friend of mine!
The sweet thought of your happiness;
The knowledge of your joy divine
Is fragrant with a power to bless.

With the day's work preoccupied,
Vaguely, half conscious of delight,
Upborne as on a buoyant tide,
I wonder why life seems so bright.

Then memory speaks, then winter gray,
The age and cares that have no end
Touch one no more. I am to-day
Rich in the wealth that cheers my friend.

—*Celia Leighton*

Fancy Fans

Eight pretty fans set off this enchanting doily.
It makes a lovely gift for a young woman with a taste for elegance!

Getting Started

Experience Level
Intermediate

Size
11½" in diameter

Materials
- Crochet cotton size 30: 350 yds white
- Size 9 steel crochet hook

Gauge
5 dc rnds = 1"; [1 dc, ch 1] 9 times = 1"

Pattern Note
Join rnds with a sl st unless otherwise stated.

Doily

Rnd 1: Ch 10, join to form a ring, ch 3 (counts as first dc), 23 dc in ring, join in 3rd ch of beg ch-3. (24 dc)

Rnd 2: Ch 7 (counts as first dc, ch 4), sk 2 dc, dc in next dc, [ch 4, sk 2 dc, dc in next dc] rep around, join in 3rd ch of beg ch-7.

Rnd 3: Sl st in next ch, ch 7 (counts as first dc, ch 4), sk 2 chs, dc, ch 1 and dc in next dc, ch 1, [dc in next ch, ch 4, sk 2 chs, dc, ch 1 and dc in next dc, ch 1] rep around, join in 3rd ch of beg ch-7.

Rnd 4: Sl st in next ch, ch 7, sk 2 chs, dc in next ch, [ch 1, dc in next ch-1 sp] twice, ch 1, *dc in next ch, ch 4, sk 2 chs, dc in next ch, [ch 1, dc in next ch-1 sp] twice, ch 1, rep from * around, join in 3rd ch of beg ch-7.

Rnd 5: Sl st in next ch, ch 7, sk 2 chs, dc in next ch, [ch 1, dc in next ch-1 sp] 3 times, ch 1, *dc in next ch, ch 4, sk 2 chs, dc in next ch, [ch 1, dc in next ch-1 sp] 3 times, ch 1, rep from * around, join in 3rd ch of beg ch-7.

Rnd 6: Sl st in next ch, ch 8, sk 2 chs, dc in next ch, [ch 1, dc in next ch-1 sp] 4 times, ch 1, *dc in next ch, ch 5, sk 2 chs, dc in next ch, [ch 1, dc in next ch-1 sp] 4 times, ch 1, rep from * around, join in 3rd ch of beg ch-8.

Rnd 7: Sl st in next ch, ch 8, sk 3 chs, dc in next ch, [ch 1, dc in next ch-1 sp] 5 times, ch 1, *dc in next ch, ch 5, sk 3 chs, dc in next ch, [ch 1, dc in next ch-1 sp] 5 times, ch 1, rep from * around, join in 3rd ch of beg ch-8.

Rnd 8: Sl st in next ch, ch 9, sk 3 chs, dc in next ch, [ch 1, dc in next ch-1 sp] 6 times, ch 1, *dc in next ch, ch 6, sk 3 chs, dc in next ch, [ch 1, dc in next ch-1 sp] 6 times, ch 1, rep from * around, join in 3rd ch of beg ch-9.

Rnd 9: Sl st in next ch, ch 9, sk 4 chs, dc in next ch, [ch 1, dc in next ch-1 sp] 7 times, ch 1, *dc in next ch, ch 6, sk 4 chs, dc in next ch, [ch 1, dc in next ch-1 sp] 7 times, ch 1, rep from * around, join in 3rd ch of beg ch-9.

Rnd 10: Sl st in next ch, ch 10, sk 4 chs, dc in next ch, [ch 1, dc in next ch-1 sp] 8 times, ch 1, *dc in next ch, ch 7, sk 4 chs, dc in next ch, [ch 1, dc in next ch-1 sp] 8 times, ch 1, rep from * around, join in 3rd ch of beg ch-10.

Rnd 11: Sl st in next ch, ch 10, sk 5 chs, dc in next ch, [ch 1, dc in ch-1 sp] 4 times, ch 3, sk 1 ch-1 sp, dc in next ch-1 sp, [ch 1, dc in next ch-1 sp] 3 times, ch 1, *dc in next ch, ch 7, sk 5 chs, dc in next ch, [ch 1, dc in ch-1 sp] 4 times, ch 3, sk 1 ch-1 sp, dc in next ch-1 sp, [ch 1, dc in next ch-1 sp] 3 times, ch 1, rep from * around, join in 3rd ch of beg ch-10.

Rnd 12: Sl st in next ch, ch 11, sk 5 chs, dc in next ch, [ch 1, dc in next ch-1 sp] 4 times, ch 3, dc in ch-3 sp, ch 3, dc in next ch-1 sp, [ch 1, dc in next ch-1 sp] 3 times, ch 1, *dc in next ch, ch 8, sk 5 chs, dc in next ch, [ch 1, dc in next ch-1 sp] 4 times, ch 3, dc in ch-3 sp, ch 3, dc in next ch-1 sp, [ch 1, dc in next ch-1 sp] 3 times, ch 1, rep from * around, join in 3rd ch of beg ch-11.

Rnd 13: Sl st in next ch, ch 11, sk 6 chs, dc in next ch, [ch 1, dc in next ch-1 sp] 4 times, ch 3, sk 2 chs, dc in next ch, ch 1, dc in dc, ch 1, dc in next ch, ch 3, dc in next ch-1 sp, [ch 1, dc in next ch-1 sp] 3 times, ch 1, *dc in next ch, ch 8, sk 6 chs, dc in next ch, [ch 1, dc in next ch-1 sp] 4 times, ch 3, sk 2 chs, dc in next ch, ch 1, dc in next dc, ch 1, dc in next ch, ch 3, dc in next ch-1 sp, [ch 1, dc in next ch-1 sp] 3 times, ch 1, rep from * around, join in 3rd ch of beg ch-11.

Rnd 14: Sl st in next ch, ch 12, sk 6 chs, dc in next ch, [ch 1, dc in next ch-1 sp] 4 times, ch 3, sk 2 chs, dc in next ch, [ch 1, dc in next ch-1 sp] twice, ch 1, dc in next ch, ch 3, dc in next ch-1 sp, [ch 1, dc in next ch-1 sp] 3 times, ch 1, *dc in next ch, ch 9, sk 6 chs, dc in next ch, [ch 1, dc in next ch-1 sp] 4 times, ch 3, sk 2 chs, dc in next ch, [ch 1, dc in next ch-1 sp] twice, ch 1, dc in next ch, ch 3, dc in next ch-1 sp, [ch 1, dc in next ch-1 sp] 3 times, ch 1, rep from * around, join in 3rd ch of beg ch-12.

Rnd 15: Sl st in next ch, ch 12, sk 7 chs, dc in next ch, [ch 1, dc in next ch-1 sp] 4 times, ch 3, sk 2 chs, dc in next ch, [ch 1, dc in next ch-1 sp] 3 times, ch 1, dc in next ch, ch 3, dc in next ch-1 sp, [ch 1, dc in next ch-1 sp] 3 times, ch 1, *dc in next ch, ch 9, sk 7 chs, dc in next ch, [ch 1, dc in next ch-1 sp] 4 times, ch 3, sk 2 chs, dc in next ch, [ch 1, dc in next ch-1 sp] 3 times, ch 1, dc in next ch, ch 3, dc in next ch-1 sp, [ch 1, dc in next ch-1 sp] 3 times, ch 1, rep from * around, join in 3rd ch of beg ch-12.

Rnd 16: Sl st in next ch, ch 13, sk 7 chs, dc in next ch, [ch 1, dc in next ch-1 sp] 4 times, ch 3, sk 2 chs, dc in next ch, [ch 1, dc in next ch-1 sp] 4 times, ch 1, dc in next ch, ch 3, dc in ch-1 sp, [ch 1, dc in next ch-1 sp] 3 times, ch 1, *dc in next ch, ch 10, sk 7 chs, dc in next ch, [ch 1, dc in next ch-1 sp] 4 times, ch 3, sk 2 chs, dc in next ch, [ch 1, dc in next ch-1 sp] 4 times, ch 1, dc in next ch, ch 3, dc in next ch-1 sp, [ch 1, dc in next ch-1 sp] 3 times, ch 1, rep from * around, join in 3rd ch of beg ch-13.

Rnd 17: Sl st in next ch, ch 13, sk 8 chs, dc in next ch, [ch 1, dc in next ch-1 sp] 4 times, ch 3, sk 2 chs, dc in next ch, [ch 1, dc in next ch-1 sp] 5 times, ch 1, dc in next ch, ch 3, dc in next ch-1 sp, [ch 1, dc in next ch-1 sp] 3 times, ch 1, *dc in next ch, ch 10, sk 8 chs, dc in next ch, [ch 1, dc in next ch-1 sp] 4 times, ch 3, sk 2 chs, dc in next ch, [ch 1, dc in next ch-1 sp] 5 times, ch 1, dc in next ch, ch 3, dc in next ch-1 sp, [ch 1, dc in next ch-1 sp] 3 times, ch 1, rep from * around, join in 3rd ch of beg ch-13.

Rnd 18: Sl st in next ch, ch 13, sk 8 chs, dc in next ch, [ch 1, dc in next ch-1 sp] 4 times, ch 3, sk 2 chs, dc in next ch, [ch 1, dc in next ch-1 sp] 6 times, ch 1, dc in next ch, ch 3, dc in next ch-1 sp, [ch 1, dc in next ch-1 sp] 3 times, ch 1, *dc in next ch, ch 10, sk 8 chs, dc in next ch, [ch 1, dc in next ch-1 sp] 4 times, ch 3, sk 2 chs, dc in next ch, [ch 1, dc in next ch-1 sp] 6 times, ch 1, dc in next ch, ch 3, dc in next ch-1 sp, [ch 1, dc in next ch-1 sp] 3 times, ch 1, rep from * around, join in 3rd ch of beg ch-13.

Rnd 19: Sl st in next ch, ch 14, sk 8 chs, dc in next ch, [ch 1, dc in next ch-1 sp] 4 times, ch 1, dc in next ch, ch 1, sk 1 ch, dc in next ch, ch 3, sk 1 ch-1 sp, dc in next ch-1 sp, [ch 1, dc in next ch-1 sp] 4 times, ch 3, sk next ch-1 sp, dc in next ch, ch 1, sk 1 ch, dc in next ch, [ch 1, dc in next ch-1 sp] 4 times, ch 1, *dc in next ch, ch 11, sk 8 chs, dc in next ch, [ch 1, dc in next ch-1 sp] 4 times, ch 1, dc in next ch, ch 1, sk 1 ch, dc in next ch, ch 3, sk 1 ch-1 sp, dc in next ch-1 sp, [ch 1, dc in next ch-1 sp] 4 times, ch 3, sk next ch-1 sp, dc in next ch, ch 1, sk 1 ch, dc in next ch, [ch 1, dc in next ch-1 sp] 4 times, ch 1, rep from * around, join in 3rd ch of beg ch-14.

Rnd 20: Sl st in next ch, ch 14, sk 9 chs, dc in next ch, [ch 1, dc in next ch-1 sp] 6 times, ch 1, dc in next ch, ch 1, sk 1 ch, dc in next ch, ch 3, sk 1 ch-1 sp, dc in next ch-1 sp, ch 1, dc in next ch-1 sp, ch 3, sk 1 ch-1 sp, dc in next ch, ch 1, sk 1 ch, dc in next ch, [ch 1, dc in next ch-1 sp] 6 times, ch 1, *dc in next ch, ch 11, sk 9 chs, dc in next ch, [ch 1, dc in next ch-1 sp] 6 times, ch 1, dc in next ch, ch 1, sk 1 ch, dc in next ch, ch 3, sk 1 ch-1 sp, dc in next ch-1 sp, ch 3, sk 1 ch-1 sp, dc in next ch, ch 1, sk 1 ch, dc in next ch, [ch 1, dc in next ch-1 sp] 6 times, ch 1, rep from * around, join in 3rd ch of beg ch-14.

Rnd 21: Sl st in each of next 4 chs, ch 13, sk 3 chs, dc in next ch, ch 6, sk 1 ch-1 sp, dc in next ch-1 sp, [ch 1, dc in next ch-1 sp] 6 times, ch 1, dc in next ch, ch 1, sk 1 ch, dc in next ch, ch 3, sk ch-1 sp, dc in next ch, ch 1, sk 1 ch, dc in next ch, [ch 1, dc in next ch-1 sp] 7 times, ch 6, sk ch-1 sp and next 3 chs, *dc in next ch, ch 10, sk 3 chs, dc in next ch, ch 6, sk 1 ch-1 sp, dc in next ch-1 sp, [ch 1, dc in next ch-1 sp] 6 times, ch 1, dc in next ch, ch 1, sk 1 ch, dc in

next ch, ch 3, sk ch-1 sp, dc in next ch, ch 1, sk 1 ch, dc in next ch, [ch 1, dc in next ch-1 sp] 7 times, ch 6, sk ch-1 sp and next 3 chs, rep from * around, join in 3rd ch of beg ch-13.

Rnd 22: Sl st in next ch, ch 4, 15 tr in ch-10 sp, ch 7, sk 1 ch-1 sp, dc in next ch-1 sp, [ch 1, dc in next ch sp] 15 times, ch 7, *16 tr in ch-10 sp, ch 7, sk 1 ch-1 sp, dc in next ch-1 sp, [ch 1, dc in next ch sp] 15 times, ch 7, rep from * around, join in 4th ch of beg ch-4.

Rnd 23: Ch 4, tr in next tr, [ch 4, tr in next 2 tr] 7 times, ch 8, sk 2 ch-1 sps, dc in next ch-1 sp, [ch 1, dc in next ch-1 sp] 10 times, ch 8, *tr in next 2 tr, [ch 4, tr in each of next 2 tr] 7 times, ch 8, sk 2 ch-1 sps, dc in next ch-1 sp, [ch 1, dc in next ch-1 sp] 10 times, ch 8, rep from * around, join in 4th ch of beg ch-4.

Rnd 24: Sl st into ch-4 sp, ch 13, sl st in 5th ch from hook for picot, ch 3, tr in next ch-4 sp, [ch 9, sl st in 5th ch from hook, ch 3, tr in sp] 5 times, ch 9, sl st in 5th ch from hook for picot, ch 3, tr in 4th ch, ch 9, sl st in 5th ch from hook, ch 3, sk 1 ch, tr in next ch, ch 6, sk 2 ch-1 sps, retaining last lp of each st on hook, tr in each of next 6 ch-1 sps, yo, draw through all lps on hook, ch 6, sk 2 ch-1 sps and next 2 chs, tr in next ch, ch 9, sl st in 5th ch from hook, ch 3, sk 1 ch, tr in next ch, ch 9, sl st in 5th ch from hook for picot, *tr in next ch-4 sp, [ch 9, sl st in 5th ch from hook, ch 3, tr in next ch-4 sp] 6 times, ch 9, sl st in 5th ch from hook for picot, ch 3, tr in 4th ch, ch 9, sl st in 5th ch from hook for picot, ch 3, sk 1 ch, tr in next ch, ch 6, sk 2 ch-1 sps, retaining last lp of each st, tr in each of next 6 ch-1 sps, yo, draw through all lps on hook, ch 6, sk 2 ch-1 sps and next 2 chs, tr in next ch, ch 9, sl st in 5th ch from hook, ch 3, sk 1 ch, tr in next ch, ch 9, sl st in 5th ch from hook, ch 3, rep from * around, join in 4th ch of beg ch-13, fasten off.

—Designed by Dorothy Newman

Classy Clusters

Rounds of delicate clusters are worked close together in the center of this doily, then are gradually spaced out, creating a lovely effect.

Getting Started

Experience Level
Beginner

Size
12" in diameter

Materials
- Crochet cotton size 10 (50 grams per ball): 1 ball blue
- Size 7 steel crochet hook

Gauge
Rnds 1–6 = 2¼" diameter

Pattern Note
Join rnds with a sl st unless otherwise stated.

Pattern Stitch
2-dc cluster (2-dc cl): Yo, insert hook in next st and draw up a lp, yo and pull through 2 lps on hook, yo, insert hook in same st and pull up a lp, yo and pull through 2 lps on hook, yo and pull through all lps on hook.

Doily

Rnd 1: Ch 6, join to form a ring, ch 5, [dc in ring, ch 2] 11 times, ch 2, join in 3rd ch of beg ch-5.

Rnd 2: Ch 1, sc in same place, ch 1, sc in first sp, *ch 1, sc in next dc, ch 1, sc in next sp, rep from * around, ending with ch 1, join in first sc. (24 sc)

Rnd 3: Ch 1, sc in same place, *ch 1, sc in next sc, rep from * around, join in first sc. (24 sc)

Rnd 4: Ch 1, sc in same place, [ch 1, sc in next sc] twice, *[ch 1, sc, ch 1, sc] in next sc (inc made), [ch 1, sc in next sc] 3 times, rep from * 4 times, ch 1, inc in next sc, ch 1, join in first sc. (30 sc)

Rnd 5: Rep Rnd 3. (30 sc)

Rnd 6: Ch 3, dc in same place, *ch 2, 2-dc cl in next sc, rep from * around, ending with ch 2, join in top of first dc. (30 2-dc cls)

Rnd 7: Ch 1, sc in same place, *ch 1, sc in next ch-2 sp, ch 1, sc in top of next cl, rep from * around, ending with ch 1, join in first sc. (60 sc)

Rnds 8–10: Rep Rnd 3. (60 sc)

Rnd 11: Rep Rnd 6. (60 2-dc cls)

Rnd 12: Sl st to first ch-2 sp, ch 3, dc in same sp, *ch 2, 2-dc cl in next ch-2 sp, rep from * around, ending with ch 2, join in top of first dc. (60 2-dc cls)

Rnds 13 & 14: Rep Rnd 12. (60 2-dc cls)

Rnds 15–17: Sl st to first ch-2 sp, ch 3, dc in same sp, *ch 3, 2-dc cl in next ch-2 sp, rep from * around, ending with ch 3, join in top of first dc.

Continued on Page 127

Wheat & Grape Doily

*Clusters of grapes among sheaves of wheat remind us
of a time of harvest and bounty, celebrated with thanksgiving.*

Getting Started

Experience Level
Intermediate

Size
16½" in diameter

Materials
- Crochet cotton size 30 (225 yds per ball):
  1 ball white
- Size 12 steel crochet hook

Gauge
4 tr = ½"

Pattern Note
Join rnds with a sl st unless otherwise stated.

Pattern Stitch
Cluster (cl): Tr in each of the next 4 tr keeping last lp of each st on hook, thread over and work off all lps at once.

Doily

Rnd 1: Ch 10, join to form a ring, ch 3 and work 23 dc in ring, join in 3rd ch of beg ch-3.

Rnd 2: [Ch 5, sk 1 dc, sc in next dc] 11 times, ch 2, dc in joining (this brings thread in position for next rnd).

Rnd 3: *Ch 7, sc in next lp, rep from * around, ending with ch 3, tr in dc.

Rnd 4: *Ch 9, sc in next lp, rep from * around, ending with ch 4, dtr in tr.

Rnd 5: Ch 4, 3 tr in dtr, [ch 7, 4 tr in center st of next lp] 11 times, ch 3, tr in 4th ch of beg ch-4.

Rnd 6: Ch 6, tr in same sp where tr was made keeping last lp of st on hook, cl, *ch 6, sc in next lp, ch 6, cl over next 4 tr, rep from * around, ending with ch 3, dc in tr.

Rnd 7: *Ch 7, sc in next lp, rep from * around, join in dc.

Rnd 8: Ch 3, 6 dc in next lp, *dc in next sc, 6 dc in next lp, rep from * around, join in 3rd ch of beg ch-3.

Rnd 9: *Ch 9, sk 6 dc, sc in next dc, rep from * around, ending with ch 4, sk 6 dc, join with dtr.

Rnd 10: *Ch 7, 4 tr in center st of next lp, ch 7, sc in next lp, rep from * around, ending with ch 3, tr in dtr.

Rnd 11: *Ch 9, sc in next lp, ch 5, tr cl over the next 4 tr, ch 5, sc in next lp, rep from * around, join in tr.

Rnd 12: Sl st to center st of next lp, ch 4, 3 tr in same sp, *ch 6, tr, ch 3, tr in next cl, ch 6, sk 1 lp, 4 tr in center st of next lp, rep from * around, ending to correspond, join in 4th ch of beg ch-4.

Rnd 13: Ch 4, tr in each of the next 3 tr keeping last lp of each st on hook, yo and work off all lps at once, *ch 5, sk 1 lp, 4 dtr in next tr, ch 2, [dtr, ch 3, dtr] in next lp, ch 2, 4 dtr in next tr, ch 5, sk 1 lp, tr cl over next 4 tr, rep from * around, ending to correspond, join in first cl.

Rnd 14: Ch 9, *dtr cl over next 4 dtr, ch 3, 4 dtr in next dtr, ch 2, [dtr, ch 3, dtr] in next lp, ch 2, 4 dtr in next dtr, ch 3, dtr cl over next 4 dtr, ch 4, dtr in next cl, ch 4, rep from * around, ending to correspond, join in 5th ch of beg ch-9.

Rnd 15: Ch 5, dtr in same sp, *ch 4, sk next cl, dtr cl over next 4 dtr, ch 3, 4 dtr in next dtr, ch 2, [dtr, ch 3, dtr] in next lp, ch 2, 4 dtr in next dtr, ch 3, dtr cl over next 4 dtr, ch 4, sk next cl, 2 dtr in next dtr, rep from * around, ending to correspond, join in 5th ch of beg ch-5.

Rnd 16: Ch 5, dtr in sp before next dtr, dtr in next dtr, *ch 5, sk next cl, dtr cl over next 4 dtr, ch 3, 4 dtr in next dtr, ch 2, dtr, ch 3, dtr in next lp, ch 2, 4 dtr in next dtr, ch 3, dtr cl over next 4 dtr, ch 5, sk next cl, dtr in next dtr, dtr in sp before next dtr, dtr in next dtr, rep from * around, ending to correspond, join in 5th ch of beg ch-5.

Rnd 17: Ch 5, dtr in same sp, dtr in next dtr, 2 dtr in next dtr, *ch 5, sk next cl, dtr cl over next 4 dtr, ch 3, 4 dtr in next dtr, ch 2, dtr, ch 3, dtr in next lp, ch 2, 4 dtr in next dtr, ch 3, dtr cl over next 4 dtr, ch 5, sk next cl, 2 dtr in next dtr, dtr in next dtr, 2 dtr in next dtr, rep from * around, ending to correspond, join in 5th ch of beg ch-5.

Rnd 18: Ch 6, dtr in same sp, *ch 1, dtr in next dtr, rep from * to within last dtr of same dtr group, ch 1, dtr, ch 1, dtr in next dtr, ch 5, sk next cl, dtr cl over next 4 dtr, ch 3, 4 dtr in next dtr, ch 2, dtr, ch 3, dtr in next lp, ch 2, 4 dtr in next dtr, ch 3, dtr cl over next 4 dtr, ch 5, sk next cl, 2 dtr with ch 1 between in next dtr, rep from * around, ending to correspond, join in 5th ch of beg ch-6.

Rnd 19: Rep Rnd 18.

Rnd 20: Ch 5, dtr in next ch-1 sp, in next dtr and in next ch-1 sp keeping last lp of each dtr on hook, yo and work off all lps at once, **ch 7, work dtr cl working in next dtr, next ch-1 lp, next dtr and next ch-1 lp, sk next dtr, *ch 7, work dtr cl working in next ch-1 lp, next dtr, next ch-1 lp, next dtr, rep from * once, ch 5, sk 1 cl, dtr cl over next 4 dtr, ch 5, sk 1 lp, 6 tr in center st of next lp, ch 5, sk 1 lp, dtr cl over next 4 dtr, ch 5, sk 1 cl, work a dtr cl working in next dtr, next ch-1 sp, next dtr and next ch-1 sp, rep from ** around in same manner, ending to correspond and ending with ch 2, dc in top of first cl.

Rnd 21: [Ch 7, sc in next lp] 5 times, *ch 7, tr cl over next 6 tr, [ch 7, sc in next lp] 7 times, rep from * around, ending with ch 3, tr in dc.

Rnds 22 & 23: *Ch 8, sc in next lp, rep from * around, ending each rnd with ch 4, tr in tr.

Rnd 24: *Ch 9, sc in next lp, rep from * around, ending with ch 4, dtr in tr.

Rnd 25: Ch 4, 3 tr in same sp, *ch 5, sc in next lp, ch 5, 4 tr in center st of next lp, rep from * around, ending to correspond, ch 5, join.

Rnd 26: Ch 4, tr in each of the next 3 tr keeping last lp of each tr on hook, yo and work off all lps at once, *ch 8, sc in next sc, ch 8, tr cl over next 4 tr, rep from * around, ending with ch 8, sc in next sc, ch 4, tr in top of first cl.

Rnd 27: *Ch 9, sc in next lp, rep from * around, ending with ch 4, dtr in tr.

Rnds 28 & 29: Rep Rnd 27 but end each rnd with ch 4, dtr in dtr.

Rnd 30: Ch 9, sl st in 3rd ch from hook for picot, ch 2, tr in same sp, *ch 5, sc in center st of next lp, ch 5, tr in center st of next lp, ch 5, sl st in 3rd ch from hook for picot, ch 2, tr in same sp, rep from * around, ending to correspond, ch 5, join in 4th ch of beg ch-9, fasten off. ❖

Classy Clusters

Continued from Page 123

Rnds 18–20: Rep Rnds 15–17, working ch 4 between cls.

Rnds 21–23: Rep Rnds 15–17, working ch 5 between cls.

Rnds 24 & 25: Rep Rnds 15 and 16, working ch 6 between cls.

Rnd 26 (Edging): Ch 1, sc in same place as sl st, *ch 5, sc in top of cl of Rnd 24 (catching ch-6 in sc), ch 5, sc in top of cl of Rnd 25, rep from * around, ending ch 5, sc in top of dc of Rnd 24, fasten off.

—Designed by Rose Pirrone

A Summer Idyl

Swinging in a shaded hammock,
Watching Phyllis at her lace,
Life seems dowered with richest promise,
Filled with tenderness and grace.

Flowers are blooming, birds are singing,
Bowered in leafy tents of green,
I have eyes for naught but Phyllis,
Busy little household queen.

In and out her shuttle flashes,
While the dainty fabric grows
Like a dream of fairy weaving.
Smooth and lustrous, row on rows.

Chains and picots, rings and roses
One by one I see arrayed,
Fashioned by the slender fingers
Of this winsome, 'witching maid.

All intent upon her tatting,
Still she sits, demure and cool,
Never once her eyes are lifted—
Deep-fringed, like a woodland pool.

How I wish I new her fancies . . .
Phyllis tilts her saucy face,
Saying sweetly, "I was thinking
My new thread makes lovely lace!"

—Allan C. Stewart

Wheels Within a Wheel

These eye-catching motifs can be worked into an antique-style doily as shown, or worked into a vintage tablecloth or runner.

Pattern Note
Join rnds with a sl st unless otherwise stated.

Motifs

First Motif (center motif)
Rnd 1 (RS): Ch 6, join to form a ring, ch 3 (counts as first dc), 23 dc in ring, join in 3rd ch of beg ch-3. (24 dc)

Note: Lp a short piece of thread around any st to mark last rnd as the right side.

Rnd 2: Ch 9, yo twice, insert hook in 7th ch from hook and pull up a lp (4 lps on hook), sk next dc, yo, insert hook in next dc and pull up a lp, [yo and draw through 2 lps on hook] 5 times (beg cross st made), ch 3, *yo 4 times, insert hook in next dc and pull up a lp (6 lps on hook), [yo and draw through 2 lps on hook] twice, sk next dc, yo, insert hook in next dc and pull up a lp (6 lps on hook), [yo and draw through 2 lps on hook] 5 times, ch 3, dc in center of cross (cross st made), ch 3, rep from * 6 more times, join in 6th ch of beg ch-9. (8 cross sts)

Rnd 3: Ch 1, 5 sc in each ch-3 sp around, join in first sc. (80 sc)

Rnds 4–8: Ch 1, sc in each sc around, join in first sc.

Rnd 9: Ch 3, dc in next sc and in each sc around, join in 3rd ch of beg ch-3.

Rnd 10: Work beg cross st, ch 3, sk next dc, [work cross st, ch 3, sk next dc] rep around, join in 6th ch of beg ch-9. (20 cross sts)

Rnd 11: Sl st in first ch-3 sp, ch 5, dc in same sp, ch 3, sc in next ch-3 sp, ch 3, *[dc, ch 2, dc] in next ch-3 sp, ch 3, sc in next ch-3 sp, ch 3, rep from * around, join in 3rd ch of beg ch-5. (20 ch-2 sps)

Rnd 12: Sl st in first ch-2 sp, ch 6, dc in same sp, ch 3, sc in next sc, ch 3, [dc, ch 3, dc] in next ch-2 sp (V-st made), ch 3, sc in next sc, ch 3, rep from * around, join in 3rd ch of beg ch-6, fasten off. (20 V-sts)

Second Motif
Rnds 1–11: Rep Rnds 1–11 of First Motif.

Rnd 12: Sl st in first ch-2 sp, ch 6, dc in same sp, ch 3, sc in next sc, ch 3, dc in next ch-2 sp, ch 1, with wrong sides tog, sl st in ch-2 sp of any V-st on First Motif, ch 1, dc in same sp on motif being worked, ch 3, sc in next sc, ch 3, [dc in next ch-2 sp, ch 1, with WS tog, sl st in ch-2 sp of next V-st on First Motif, ch 1, dc in same sp on motif being worked, ch 3, sc in next sc, ch 3] 3 times, [work V-st, ch 3, sc in next sc, ch 3] rep around, join in 3rd ch of beg ch-6, fasten off.

Third Motif

Rnds 1–11: Rep Rnds 1–11 of First Motif.

Rnd 12: Sl st in first ch-2 sp, ch 6, dc in same sp, ch 3, sc in next sc, ch 3, dc in next ch-2 sp, ch 1, with WS tog, sl st in ch-2 sp of 3rd V-st from last joining on motif just worked, ch 1, dc in same sp on motif being worked, ch 3, sc in next sc, ch 3, [dc in next ch-2 sp, ch 1, with WS tog, sl st in ch-2 sp of next V-st on motif just worked, ch 1, dc in same sp on motif being worked, ch 3, sc in next sc, ch 3] twice, [dc in next ch-2 sp, ch 1, with WS tog, sl st in next free ch-2 sp on First Motif, ch 1, dc in same sp of motif being worked, ch 3, sc in next sc, ch 3] 3 times, [work V-st, ch 3, sc in next sc, ch 3] rep around, join in 3rd ch of beg ch-6, fasten off.

Fourth Motif

Rnds 1–11: Rep Rnds 1–11 of First Motif.

Rnd 12: Sl st in first ch-2 sp, ch 6, dc in same sp, ch 3, sc in next sc, ch 3, dc in next ch-2 sp, ch 1, with WS tog, sl st in ch-2 sp of 3rd V-st from last joining on motif just worked, ch 1, dc in same sp on motif being worked, ch 3, sc in next sc, ch 3, [dc in next ch-2 sp, ch 1, with WS tog, sl st in ch-2 sp of next V-st on motif just worked, ch 1, dc in same sp on motif being worked, ch 3, sc in next sc, ch 3] twice, [dc in next ch-2 sp, ch 1, with WS tog, sl st in next free ch-2 sp on First Motif, ch 1, dc in same sp on motif being worked, ch 3, sc in next sc, ch 3] 4 times, [work V-st, ch 3, sc in next sc, ch 3] rep around, join in 3rd ch of beg

ch-6, fasten off.

Fifth Motif

Rnds 1–11: Rep Rnds 1–11 of First Motif.

Rnd 12: Sl st in first ch-2 sp, ch 6, dc in same sp, ch 3, sc in next sc, ch 3, dc in next ch-2 sp, ch 1, with WS tog, sl st in ch-2 sp of 2nd V-st from last joining on motif just worked, ch 1, dc in same sp on motif being worked, ch 3, sc in next sc, ch 3, dc in next ch-2 sp, ch 1, with WS tog, sl st in ch-2 sp of next V-st on motif just worked, ch 1, dc in same sp on motif being worked, ch 3, sc in next sc, ch 3, dc in next ch-2 sp, ch 1, with WS tog, sl st in next joining, ch 1, dc in same sp on motif being worked, ch 3, sc in next sc, ch 3, [dc in next ch-2 sp, ch 1, with WS tog, sl st in next free ch-2 sp on First Motif, ch 1, dc in same sp on motif being worked, ch 3, sc in next sc, ch 3] 3 times, [work V-st, ch 3, sc in next sc, ch 3] rep around, join in 3rd ch of beg ch-6, fasten off.

Sixth Motif

Work same as Third Motif.

Seventh Motif

Rnds 1–11: Rep Rnds 1–11 of First Motif.

Rnd 12 (Joining Rnd): Sl st in first ch-2 sp, ch 6, dc in same sp, ch 3, sc in next sc, ch 3, dc in next ch-2 sp, ch 1, with WS tog, sl st in ch-2 sp of 3rd V-st from last joining on motif just worked, ch 1, dc in same sp on motif being worked, ch 3, sc in next sc, ch 3, [dc in next ch-2 sp, ch 1, with WS tog, sl st in ch-2 sp of next V-st on motif just worked, ch 1, dc in same sp on motif being worked, ch 3, sc in next sc, ch 3] twice, [dc in next ch-2 sp, ch 1, with WS tog, sl st in next free ch-2 sp on First Motif, ch 1, dc in same sp on motif being worked, ch 3, sc in next sc, ch 3] 3 times, dc in next ch-2 sp, ch 1, with WS tog, sl st in next joining, ch 1, dc in same sp on motif being worked, ch 3, sc in next sc, ch 3, [dc in next ch-2 sp, ch 1, with WS tog, sl st in next free ch-2 sp on Second Motif, ch 1, dc in same sp on motif being worked, ch 3, sc in next sc, ch 3] twice, [work V-st, ch 3, sc in next sc, ch 3] rep around, join in 3rd ch of beg ch-6, do not fasten off.

Edging

Rnd 1: Ch 1, 3 sc in first ch-3 sp, 2 sc in next ch-3 sp, sc in next sc on Rnd 11, *+[2 sc in next ch-3 sp] twice, sc in next joining, [2 sc in next ch-3 sp] twice, sc in next sc on Rnd 11 +, [2 sc in next ch-3 sp, 3 sc in next ch-3 sp, 2 sc in next ch-3 sp, sc in next sc on Rnd 11] 11 times, rep from * 4 times more, then rep from + to + once, 2 sc in next ch-3 sp, [3 sc in next ch-3 sp, 2 sc in next ch-3 sp, sc in next sc on Rnd 11, 2 sc in next ch-3 sp] 10 times, join in first sc.

Rnd 2: Sl st across to first joining, ch 4, sk next 8 sc, dtr in next sc, *+ch 10, [yo 3 times, insert hook in same sc and pull up a lp, {yo and draw through 2 lps on hook} 3 times, sk next 7 sc, yo 3 times, insert hook in next sc and pull up a lp, {yo and draw through 2 lps on hook} 3 times, yo and draw through all 3 lps on hook (dec made)], ch 10, [dec, ch 10] 9 times +, yo 3 times, insert hook in same sc and pull up a lp, [yo and draw through 2 lps on hook] 3 times, [sk next 8 sc, yo 3 times, insert hook in next sc and pull up a lp, {yo and draw through 2 lps on hook} 3 times] twice, yo and draw through all 4 lps on hook (double dec made), rep from * 4 times more, then rep from + to + once, dtr in same sc, join in 4th ch of beg ch-4. (66 ch-10 sps)

Rnd 3: Ch 1, sc in same st, 10 sc in next ch-10 sp, [sc in next dec, 10 sc in next ch-10 sp] rep around, join in first sc. (726 sc)

Rnd 4: Sl st in next 3 sc, ch 1, sc in next 117 sc, [sk next 4 sc, sc in next 117 sc] 5 times, sk next 2 sc, join in first sc. (702 sc)

Rnd 5: Sl st in next 2 sc, ch 1, sc in next 114 sc, [sk next 3 sc, sc in next 114 sc] 5 times, sk last 2 sc, join in first sc. (684 sc)

Rnd 6: Sl st in next 6 sc, ch 1, hdc in next sc (beg hdc dec made), *+ch 4, sk next 4 sc, [tr, ch 3, tr] in next sc, ch 4, sk next 4 sc, [{yo, insert hook in next sc and pull up a lp} twice, yo and draw through all 5 lps on hook (hdc dec made)], ch 4, [sk next 4 sc, {tr, ch 3, tr} in next sc, ch 3, sk next 4 sc, work hdc dec, ch 4] 8 times, sk next 6 sc, [tr, ch 3, tr] in next sc, ch 4, sk next 6 sc +, work hdc dec, rep from * 4 times more, then rep from + to + once, join in beg dec.

Rnd 7: Sl st across to first ch-3 sp, ch 7, tr in same sp, ch 4, *+[sc in next dec, ch 4, sk next ch-4 sp, {tr, ch 3, tr} in next ch-3 sp, ch 4] 8 times, sk next 2 ch-4 sps, sc in next ch-3 sp, ch 4, sk next 2 ch-4 sps +, [tr, ch 3, tr] in next ch-3 sp, ch 4, rep from * 4 times more, then rep from + to + once, join in 4th ch of beg ch-7.

Rnd 8: Ch 1, *[2 sc, ch 2, 2 sc] in next ch-3 sp, 4 sc in next ch-4 sp, sc in next sc, 4 sc in next ch-4 sp, rep from * around, join in first sc, fasten off.

—Designed by Ann Kirtley

Twinkling Stars

Capture the beauty of a starry night with a cheerful star doily. From vibrant sunbursts and stars to a six-pointed Star of David and gentle swirls, the designs included will inspire you to reach new heights of crochet.

Pretty Swirls

Daydream Doily

Menorah Doily

Sunburst Surprise

Doily of Stars

Pretty Swirls

Dress up a plain table with this small accent doily featuring eye-catching swirls spinning outward!

Getting Started

Experience Level
Beginner

Size
10½" in diameter

Materials
- Crochet cotton size 30 (225 yds per ball): 1 ball white
- Size 10 steel crochet hook

Gauge
6 dc = ½"; 4 dc rnds = ¾"

Pattern Note
Join rnds with a sl st unless otherwise stated.

Doily

Rnd 1: Ch 7, join to form a ring, ch 5, dc in ring, [ch 2, dc in ring] 8 times, ch 2, join in 3rd ch of beg ch-5. (10 dc)

Rnd 2: Ch 3, dc in same st, ch 3, [2 dc in next dc, ch 3] rep around, join.

Rnd 3: Sl st into ch-3 sp, [ch 6, sc in next ch sp] rep around to within last sp, ch 4, join with dc in base of starting ch. (10 ch lps)

Rnd 4: Ch 3, 4 dc in same ch sp, ch 3, [5 dc in next ch sp, ch 3] rep around, join in 3rd ch of beg ch-3.

Rnd 5: Sl st in next 2 dc, ch 3, dc in each of next 2 dc, 4 dc in ch sp, ch 3, [sk 2 dc, dc in each of next 3 dc, 4 dc in ch sp, ch 3] rep around, join.

Rnd 6: Sl st in next 2 dc, ch 3, dc in each dc to within ch sp, 4 dc in ch sp, ch 3, [sk 2 dc, dc in each dc to within ch sp, 4 dc in ch sp, ch 3] rep around, join.

Rnds 7–10: Rep Rnd 6.

At the end of Rnd 10 there will be a total of 17 dc between each ch-3 lp. (170 dc and 10 ch-3 lps)

Rnd 11: Sl st in next 2 sts, ch 3, dc in each of next 14 dc, ch 2, dc in ch-3 lp, ch 2, [sk 2 dc, dc in each of next 15 dc, ch 2, dc in ch-3 lp, ch 2] rep around, join.

Rnd 12: Sl st in next 2 sts, ch 3, dc in each of next 12 dc, ch 2, V-st of dc, ch 2, dc in single dc in ch lp, ch 2, [sk 2 dc, dc in each of next 13 dc, ch 2, V-st of dc, ch 2, dc in single dc in ch lp, ch 2] rep around, join.

Rnd 13: Sl st in next 2 sts, ch 3, dc in each of next 10 dc, ch 5, 3 sc in ch-1 sp of V-st, ch 5, [sk 2 dc, dc in each of next 11 dc, ch 5, 3 sc in ch-1 sp of V-st, ch 5] rep around, join.

Rnd 14: Sl st in next 2 sts, ch 3, dc in each of next 8 dc, ch 4, sc in first ch lp, ch 4, dc in middle sc of 3-sc group, ch 4, sc in next ch lp, ch 4, [sk 2 dc, dc in each of next 9 dc, ch 4, sc in first ch lp, ch 4, dc in middle sc of 3-sc group, ch 4, sc in next ch lp, ch 4] rep around, join.

Continued on Page 139

Daydream Doily

This exquisite doily is a masterpiece of beautiful crochet design. Created in 1944 by an unknown designer, it will be a jewel in your doily collection.

Getting Started

Experience Level
Intermediate

Size
Approximately 17½" in diameter

Materials
• Tatting cotton size 20 (106 yds per ball): 4 balls
• Size 9 steel crochet hook

Gauge
6 sc = ½"

Pattern Notes

For a larger doily, use heavier thread and appropriate hook.

Join rnds with a sl st unless otherwise stated.

Doily

Rnd 1: Starting at center, ch 10, join to form a ring, ch 1, 16 sc in ring, join in first sc. (16 sc in ring)

Rnd 2: Sc in same sc as sl st, [ch 5, sk next sc, sc in next sc] 7 times, ch 5. (8 ch-5 sps)

Rnd 3: [Sc in next sc, 2 sc in ch-5 sp, ch 5] 8 times.

Rnds 4–17: [Sk first sc, sc in rem sc of group, 2 sc in ch-5 lp, ch 5] 8 times. (17 sc in sc group at end of Rnd 17)

Rnd 18: [Sk first sc of sc group, sc in each of next 15 sc, ch 5, sc in ch-5 lp, ch 5] 8 times.

Rnd 19: *Sk first sc of sc group, sc in each of next 13 sc, [ch 5, sc in next ch-5 lp] twice, ch 5, rep from * around.

Rnds 20–25: *Sk first sc of sc group, sc to last sc of group, [ch 5, sc] in each ch-5 lp, ch 5, rep from * around, at end of Rnd 25 sc in next ch-5 lp. (1 sc remains of each sc group with 9 ch-5 lps between)

Rnds 26–30: *Ch 6, sc in next lp, rep from * around. (72 ch-6 lps)

Rnd 31: [Ch 6, sc in next lp] rep to within lp directly above point of sc group, *ch 6, 9 dc in next ch-6 lp, [ch 6, sc in next ch-6 lp] 8 times, rep from * around, ending with 9 dc in lp directly over point. (8 groups of 9 dc directly over point of sc group)

Rnd 32: *[Ch 6, sc in next ch-6 lp] rep to within dc group, ch 6, sk next 4 dc, sc in next dc, ch 6, sc in next ch-6 lp, rep from * around. (80 ch-6 lps)

Rnds 33 & 34: *Ch 6, sc in next ch-6 lp, rep from * around.

Rnd 35: Sl st into ch-6 lp, ch 5 (counts as first hdc, ch 3), *2 hdc in next ch-6 lp, ch 3, rep from * around, ending with hdc in same ch lp as beg ch-5, sl st to join in 2nd ch of beg ch-5. (80 ch-3 sps)

Rnd 36: Ch 2, *2 hdc in ch-3 sp, hdc in next 2 hdc, rep from * around, join in 2nd ch of beg ch-2. (320 hdc)

Rnd 37: Ch 1, *[sc in each of next 17 hdc, ch 4, sk next 4 hdc, 2 dc, ch 2, 2 dc in next hdc (shell), ch 4, sk next 4 hdc] twice, sc in each of next 17 hdc, ch 4, sk next 5 hdc, [2 dc, ch 2, 2 dc] in next hdc, ch 4, sk next 5 hdc, rep from * around, join in first sc. (12 groups of 17 sc with shell between)

Rnd 38: Sl st in next sc, ch 1, sc in same place, sc in each of next 14 sc, sk last sc, *ch 4, [shell, ch 2, shell] in next ch-2 shell sp (3 ch-2 sps), ch 4, sk next sc, sc in each of next 15 sc, rep from * around, ending last rep with ch 4, join in first sc.

Rnd 39: Sl st in next sc, ch 1, sc in same place, sc in each of next 12 sc, sk last sc, *ch 4, [shell in next ch-2 sp, ch 3] twice, shell in next ch-2 sp, ch 4, sk next sc, sc in each of next 13 sc, rep from * around, ending last rep with ch 4, join in first sc.

Rnd 40: Sl st in next sc, ch 1, sc in same place, sc in each of next 10 sc, sk last sc, *ch 4, shell in next ch-2 shell sp, ch 3, [shell, ch 2, shell] in next ch-2 shell sp, ch 3, shell in next ch-2 shell sp, ch 4, sk next sc, sc in each of next 11 sc, rep from * around, ending last rep with ch 4, join in first sc.

Rnd 41: Sl st in next sc, ch 1, sc in same place, sc in each of next 8 sc, sk last sc, *ch 5, shell in next ch-2 shell sp, ch 3, [shell in next ch-2 sp, ch 2] twice, shell in next ch-2 sp, ch 3, shell in next ch-2 shell sp, ch 5, sk next sc, sc in each of next 9 sc, rep from * around, ending last rep with ch 5, join in first sc.

Rnd 42: Sl st in next sc, ch 1, sc in same place, sc in each of next 6 sc, sk last sc, *ch 5, [shell in next ch-2 shell sp, ch 3] twice, [shell, ch 2, shell] in next ch-2 shell sp, [ch 3, shell in next ch-2 shell sp] twice, ch 5, sk next sc, sc in each of next 7 sc, rep from * around, ending last rep with ch 5, join in first sc.

Rnd 43: Sl st in next sc, ch 1, sc in same place, sc in each of next 4 sc, sk last sc, *ch 5, shell in next ch-2 shell sp, ch 4, shell in next ch-2 shell sp, [ch 3, shell in next ch-2 sp] 3 times, ch 3, shell in next ch-2 shell sp, ch 4, shell in next ch-2 shell sp, ch 5, sk next sc, sc in each of next 5 sc, rep from * around, ending last rep with ch 5, join in first sc.

Rnd 44: Sl st in next sc, ch 1, sc in same place, sc in each of next 2 sc, sk last sc, *ch 5, shell in next ch-2 shell sp, ch 4, [shell in next ch-2 shell sp, ch 3] twice, [shell, ch 2, shell] in next ch-2 sp, [ch 3, shell in next ch-2 shell sp] twice, ch 4, shell in next ch-2 shell sp, ch 5, sk next sc, sc in each of next 3 sc, rep from * around, ending last rep with ch 5, join in first sc.

Rnd 45: Sl st in next sc, ch 1, sc in same place, sk next sc, *ch 5, [shell in next ch-2 shell sp, ch 4] 3 times, [shell in next ch-2 sp, ch 3] twice, shell in next ch-2 sp, [ch 4, shell in next ch-2 shell sp] 3 times, ch 5, sk next sc, sc in next sc, rep from * around, ending last rep with ch 5, join in first sc.

Rnd 46: Sl st to ch-2 sp of first shell, ch 8, sl st in 4th ch from hook (picot), ch 1, dc in same shell sp, *ch 2, sc in next ch-4 sp (between shells), ch 2, [dc, ch 1, picot, ch 1, dc] in next ch-2 shell sp, rep from * across 1 point, end with [dc, ch 1, picot, ch 1, dc] in ch-2 sp of last shell of point, sk next [ch-5, sc, ch-5], [dc, ch 1, picot, ch 1, dc] in ch-2 sp of first shell of next point, rep from first * around, ending with a sl st in 3rd ch of ch-8, fasten off. ❖

Pretty Swirls

Continued from Page 135

Rnd 15: Sl st in next 2 sts, ch 3, dc in each of next 6 dc, [ch 4, sc in next ch lp] 4 times, ch 4, *sk 2 dc, dc in each of next 7 dc, [ch 4, sc in next ch lp] 4 times, ch 4, rep from * around, join.

Rnd 16: Sl st in next 2 sts, ch 3, dc in each of next 4 sts, [ch 4, sc in next ch lp] 5 times, ch 4, *sk 2 dc, dc in each of next 5 dc, [ch 4, sc in next ch lp] 5 times, ch 4, rep from * around, join.

Rnd 17: Sl st in next 2 sts, ch 3, dc in each of next 2 dc, [ch 4, dc in next ch lp] 6 times, ch 4, *sk 2 dc, dc in each of next 3 dc, [ch 4, dc in next ch lp] 6 times, ch 4, rep from * around, join.

Rnd 18: Sl st across dc sts into next ch lp, [ch 6, sc in next ch lp] rep around, ending with ch 3, dc in starting ch to join.

Note: *The ending [ch 3, dc in starting ch] sets you up in the middle of the ch lp to work the following rnd.*

Rnds 19–22: [Ch 6, sc in next ch lp] rep around, ending with ch 3, dc in starting ch to join.

Rnd 23: Ch 3, 2 dc in same ch lp, ch 3, [3 dc in next ch lp, ch 3] rep around, join in 3rd ch of beg ch-3.

Rnd 24: Ch 1, sc in same st, sc in each of next 2 dc, ch 4, [sc in each of next 3 dc, ch 4] rep around, join.

Rnd 25: Sl st into next sc, ch 1, sc in same st, ch 3, 3 dc in ch sp, ch 3, [sk 1 sc, sc in next sc, ch 3, 3 dc in ch sp, ch 3] rep around, join.

Rnd 26: Sl st into top of first dc, ch 1, sc in same st, sc in each of next 2 dc, ch 6, [sc in each of next 3 dc, ch 6] rep around, join.

Rnd 27: Sl st into next sc, ch 1, sc in same st, ch 5, retaining last lp of each dc on hook, work 2 dc in next ch lp, yo, draw through all lps on hook for cluster, ch 3, sl st in top of cluster, ch 5, [sk 1 sc, sc in next sc, ch 5, retaining last lp of each dc on hook, work 2 dc in next ch lp, yo, draw through all lps on hook for cluster, ch 3, sl st in top of cluster, ch 5] rep around, join, fasten off.

—Designed by Rose Beckett

A Patch of Sun

I opened up my cedar chest
One rainy April day,
And there I found a thousand dreams
Of travel, laid away.

I'd ironed each dream so tenderly
And packed each one with care;
I'd made a wish upon a star
And said a little prayer.

How could my dreams have wrinkled then?
And colors once so bright,

How could their sheen have faded with
The lid shut up so tight?

I took each dream from hiding, and
I smoothed with all my might;
"I know what's wrong with you," I said,
"You need a bit of light."

I took them to the window where
A patch of sun broke through;
The unaccustomed brightness made
My dreams as good as new.

—June Masters Bacher

Menorah Doily

*A Star of David design is the focal point of this traditional doily.
Let it decorate the table under a lit candelabrum.*

Getting Started

Experience Level
Intermediate

Size
15" in diameter

Materials
- Crochet cotton size 10 (325 yds per ball): 1 ball white
- Size 11 steel crochet hook

Gauge
9 dc = 1"; 3 dc rnds = 7"

Pattern Note
Join rnds with a sl st unless otherwise stated.

Doily

Rnd 1: Ch 5, join to form a ring, ch 1, 12 sc in ring, ch 1. (12 dc)

Rnd 2: Sc in same sc as beg ch-1, ch 3, sk 1 sc, [sc in next sc, ch 3, sk 1 sc] rep around, join in beg sc, ch 1.

Rnd 3: Sc in same sc as beg ch-1, ch 5, [sc in next sc, ch 5] rep around, join in beg sc, ch 1.

Rnd 4: Sc in same sc as beg ch-1, ch 7, [sc in next sc, ch 7] rep around, join in beg sc, ch 1.

Rnd 5: Sc in same sc as beg ch-1, [sc, hdc, 2 dc, ch 3, 2 dc, hdc, sc] over next ch-7 lp, [sc in next sc, sc, hdc, 2 dc, ch 3, 2 dc, hdc and sc over next ch-7 lp] rep around, join, ch 1.

Rnd 6: Sc in each st around, working [sc, ch 3, sc] in each ch-3 sp, join, ch 1.

Rnd 7: Sc, ch 3 and sc in same sc as beg ch-1, ch 3, sk 2 sc, sc in next sc, ch 3, sk 2 sc, sc, ch 3 and sc in next ch-3 sp, ch 3, sk 2 sc, sc in next sc, ch 3, sk 2 sc, [sc, ch 3 and sc in next sc, ch 3, sk 2 sc, sc in next sc, ch 3, sk 2 sc, sc, ch 3 and sc in next ch-3 sp, ch 3, sk 2 sc, sc in next sc, ch 3, sk 2 sc] rep around, join in beg sc, sl st into next ch-3 sp.

Rnd 8: Ch 4 (counts as first tr), tr, ch 2 and 2 tr in same ch-3 sp, ch 4, sk 2 ch-3 sps, sc in next ch-3 sp at point, ch 4, sk 2 ch-3 sps, [2 tr, ch 2 and 2 tr in next ch-3 sp between points, ch 4, sk 2 ch-3 sps, sc in next ch-3 sp at point, ch 4, sk 2 ch-3 sps] rep around, join in 4th ch of beg ch-4, ch 1.

Rnd 9: Sc in same st as beg ch-1, [sc in each tr, 2 sc in each ch-2 sp, 4 sc over each ch-4 sp and sc, ch 2 and sc in each sc] rep around, join in beg sc.

Rnd 10: Ch 3 (counts as first dc), dc in each sc around, working [dc, ch 2, dc] in each ch-2 sp, join in 3rd ch of beg ch-3, ch 1.

Rnd 11: Sc in each dc around, working [sc, ch 2, sc] in each ch-2 sp, join in beg sc.

Rnd 12: Ch 3 (counts as first dc), dc in each sc around, working at each ch-2 sp, ch 3, sc in ch-2 sp, ch 3, join in 3rd ch of beg ch-3.

Note: Rnd 12 has 6 dc panels each containing 20 dc sts.

On the following 9 rnds (Rnds 13–21), sk first and last dc of each panel, work 1 dc in each rem dc. For several rnds the first panel begins in the middle; simply ch 3, dc across to within last st of this panel and sk the last dc, when ending the beg panel, sk the first dc, dc across rem sts, join.

Ch 3 (counts as first dc) to beg each rnd and join in 3rd ch of beg ch-3.

Rnd 13: *Skipping first and last dc sts of each panel, dc across, [ch 3, sc in next ch-3 sp] twice, ch 3, rep from * around, join. (18 dc each panel)

Rnd 14: *Skipping first and last dc sts of each panel, dc across, [ch 3, sc in next ch-3 sp] 3 times, ch 3, rep from * around, join. (16 dc each panel)

Rnd 15: *Skipping first and last dc sts of each panel, dc across, [ch 4, sc in next ch-3 sp] 4 times, ch 4, rep from * around, join. (14 dc each panel)

Rnd 16: *Skipping first and last dc sts of each panel, dc across, [ch 4, sc in next ch-4 sp] 5 times, ch 4, rep from * around, join. (12 dc each panel)

Rnd 17: *Skipping first and last dc sts of each panel, dc across, [ch 4, sc in next ch-4 sp] 6 times, ch 4, rep from * around, join. (10 dc each panel)

Rnd 18: *Skipping first and last dc sts of each panel, dc across, [ch 4, sc in next ch-4 sp] 7 times, ch 4, rep from * around, join. (8 dc each panel)

Rnd 19: *Skipping first and last dc sts of each panel, dc across, [ch 6, sc in next ch-4 sp] 8 times, ch 6, rep from * around, join. (6 dc each panel)

Rnd 20: *Skipping first and last dc sts of each panel, dc across, [ch 6, sc in next ch-5 sp] 9 times, ch 6, rep from around, join. (4 dc each panel)

Rnd 21: *Skipping first and last dc sts of each panel, dc across, [ch 5, sc in next ch-5 sp] 10 times, ch 6, rep from * around, ending ch 2, dc in 3rd ch of beg ch-3 to join. (2 dc each panel)

Rnd 22: Ch 1, sc in same sp as beg ch-1, [ch 5, sc in next ch sp] rep around, ending ch 2, dc in beg sc.

Rnd 23: Ch 1, sc in same ch sp, ch 1, shell of 3 dc, ch 3 and 3 dc in next ch sp, ch 1, [sc in next ch sp, ch 1, shell of 3 dc, ch 3 and 3 dc in next ch sp, ch 1] rep around, join.

Rnd 24: Ch 3, 2 dc, ch 3 and 3 dc in same sc as beg ch-3, ch 2, sc in next ch-3 sp of shell, ch 2, [shell of 3 dc, ch 3 and dc in next sc, ch 2, sc in next ch-3 sp of shell, ch 2] rep around, join.

Rnd 25: Sl st into ch-3 sp of shell, ch 1, [sc, ch 3 and sc in ch-3 sp of shell, ch 3, sc in next ch-2 sp, ch 3, sc in next ch-2 sp, ch 3] rep around, join.

Rnd 26: Sl st into ch-3 sp, ch 1, [sc in ch-3 sp above shell sp, ch 5, sk next ch-3 sp, dc in next ch-3 sp, ch 5, sk next ch-3 sp] rep around, join.

Rnd 27: Sl st into ch-5 sp, ch 3, 5 dc in same ch-5 sp, ch 1, [6 dc in next ch-5 sp, ch 1] rep around, join, ch 1, turn.

Rnd 28: Sc in ch-1 sp, ch 5, [sc in next ch-1 sp, ch 5] rep around, join, turn, sl st in next ch-5 sp.

Rnd 29: [Ch 3, 2 dc, ch 3, 3 dc] in same ch-5 sp, ch 3, sc in next ch-5 sp, ch 3, [work shell of 3 dc, ch 3, 3 dc in next ch-5 sp, ch 3, sc in next ch-5 sp, ch 3] rep around, join in 3rd ch of beg ch-3.

Rnd 30: Sl st into ch-3 sp of shell, ch 1, *[sc, ch 3, sc] in ch-3 sp of shell, [ch 3, sc in next ch-

3 sp] twice, ch 3, rep from * around, join.

Rnd 31: Sl st into ch-3 sp (ch-3 sp above shell), ch 1, [sc, ch 3, sc, ch 5, sc, ch 3 and sc in ch-3 sp above shell, ch 2, sc in next ch-3 sp, ch 2, sc, ch 4, sl st in first ch and sc in next ch-3 sp, ch 2, sc in next ch-3 sp, ch 2] rep around, join, fasten off.

—Designed by Katherine Eng

Mother o' Mine

I close my eyes and a vision comes—
The old home nestled among the hills.
Where the robin sings and the wild bee hums
And the air with the breath of lilacs fills.
Wide the door with a welcome stands,
And there, enframed by the dropping vine,
With a tender smile and outstretched hands
Is Mother o' mine.

Never an idle moment spent,
Always busy with helpful things,
Mending in little frocks each rent,
Kissing away each hurt that stings,
Patiently guiding the fingers small,
Striving with stitches that twist and twine,
Never minding the ones let fall—
Dear Mother o' mine.

Ever ready with loving care
To smooth and straighten the tangled skein
Of my childhood woes, and make life fair
With the sunshine of gladness once again.
Pointing the ways that ran not quite true
With gentle caution and line on line,
All that I may be I owe to you,
O Mother o' mine!

—Alicia Carew Stewart

Sunburst Surprise

Like the pleasant surprise of the sun shining through on a stormy day, so this pretty yellow doily will delight you as it fills a corner of your home with cheerful crochet!

Getting Started

Experience Level
Intermediate

Size
11½" in diameter

Materials
- Crochet cotton size 10: 1 ball yellow
- Size 7 steel crochet hook

Gauge
8 dc and 4 rows = 1"

Pattern Note
Join rnds with a sl st unless otherwise stated.

Doily

Rnd 1: Ch 6, join to form a ring, ch 5, *dc in ring, ch 3, rep from * 6 times, join in 2nd ch of beg ch-5. (8 spokes)

Rnd 2: Ch 3, 2 dc in joining ch, *ch 3, 3 dc in next dc, rep from * around, ending ch 2, join.

Rnd 3: Ch 3, dc in joining ch, dc in next dc, 2 dc in next dc, ch 3, *2 dc in next dc, dc in next dc, 2 dc in next dc, ch 3, rep from * around, ending ch 3, join.

Rnd 4: Ch 3, dc in joining ch, *dc in each of next 3 dc, 2 dc in next dc, ch 3, 2 dc in next dc, rep from * around, ending ch 3, join.

Rnd 5: Ch 3, dc in joining ch, *dc in each of next 5 dc, 2 dc in next dc, ch 3, 2 dc in next dc, rep from * around, ending ch 3, join.

Rnd 6: Ch 3, dc in joining ch, *dc in each of next 7 dc, 2 dc in next dc, ch 3, 2 dc in next dc, rep from * around, ending ch 3, join.

Rnd 7: Ch 3, dc in joining ch, *dc in each of next 4 dc, ch 1, sk 1 st, dc in each of next 4 dc, 2 dc in next dc, ch 3, 2 dc in next dc, rep from * around, ending ch 3, join.

Rnd 8: Ch 3, dc in joining ch, *dc in each of next 5 dc, ch 1, sk ch-1, dc in each of next 5 dc, 2 dc in next dc, ch 3, 2 dc in next dc, rep from * around, ending ch 3, join.

Rnd 9: Ch 3, dc in joining ch, *dc in each of next 6 dc, ch 1, dc in each of next 6 dc, 2 dc in next dc, ch 3, 2 dc in next dc, rep from * around, ending ch 3, join.

Rnd 10: Ch 3, dc over first 2 dc, *dc in each of next 6 dc, ch 1, dc in each of next 6 dc, dec over last 2 dc, ch 4, dec over next 2 dc, rep from * around, ending ch 4, join.

Rnd 11: Ch 3, dc over first 2 dc, *dc in each of next 5 dc, ch 1, dc in each of next 5 dc, dec over next 2 dc, ch 8, rep from * around, ending ch 8, join.

Rnd 12: Ch 3, *dec over first 2 dc, dc in each of next 4 dc, ch 1, dc in each of next 4 dc, dec over next 2 dc, ch 10, rep from * around, ending ch 10, join.

Rnd 13: Ch 3, *dec over first 2 dc, dc in

Continued on Page 149

Doily of Stars

With a pristine star in the center and a delicate fan edging,
this airy doily will always hold a cherished place in your home.

Pattern Note

Join rnds with a sl st unless otherwise stated.

Doily

Rnd 1: Ch 8, join to form a ring, ch 3 (counts as first dc), 15 dc in ring, join. (16 dc)

Rnd 2: Ch 3, dc in same st, ch 1, sk 1 dc, [2 dc in next dc, ch 1, sk 1 dc] rep around, join.

Rnd 3: Ch 3, dc in same st, 2 dc in next st, ch 1, [2 dc in each of next 2 dc, ch 1] rep around, join. (32 dc)

Rnds 4–8: Ch 3, dc in same dc, dc in each dc across to within last dc, 2 dc in last dc, ch 1, [2 dc in next dc, dc in each dc across to within last dc, 2 dc in last dc, ch 1] 7 times, join. (At end of Rnd 8 you will have 14 dc across each dc group.)

Rnd 9: Sl st into 2nd dc, ch 3, dc in each of next 11 dc, ch 2, dc in ch-1 sp, ch 2, [sk 1 dc, dc in each of next 12 dc, ch 2, 1 dc over ch-1 sp, ch 2] rep around, join.

Rnd 10: Sl st to 2nd dc, ch 3, dc in each of next 9 dc, [ch 2, dc in ch-2 sp] twice, ch 2, *sk next dc, dc in each of next 10 dc, [ch 2, dc in ch-2 sp] twice, ch 2, rep from * around, join.

Rnd 11: Sl st to 2nd dc, ch 3, dc in each of next 7 dc, [ch 2, dc in ch-2 sp] 3 times, ch 2, *sk 1 dc, dc in each of next 8 dc, [ch 2, dc in next ch-2 sp] 3 times, ch 2, rep from * around, join.

Rnd 12: Sl st to 2nd dc, ch 3, dc in each of next 5 dc, [ch 3, dc in next ch-2 sp] 4 times, ch 3, *sk 1 dc, dc in each of next 6 dc, [ch 3, dc in next ch-2 sp] 4 times, ch 3, rep from * around, join.

Rnd 13: Sl st to 2nd dc, ch 3, dc in each of next 3 dc, [ch 3, dc in ch-3 sp] 5 times, ch 3, *sk 1 dc, dc in each of next 4 dc, [ch 3, dc in next ch-3 sp] 5 times, ch 3, rep from * around, join.

Rnd 14: Sl st to 2nd dc, ch 3, dc in next dc, [ch 3, dc in ch-3 sp] 6 times, ch 3, *sk 1 dc, dc in each of next 2 dc, [ch 3, dc in next ch-3 sp] 6 times, ch 3, rep from * around, join.

Rnd 15: Sl st to next ch sp, ch 6 (counts as 1 dc, ch 3), [dc in next ch-3 sp, ch 3] rep around, join in 3rd ch of beg ch-6.

Rnd 16: Sl st into ch-3 sp, ch 1, [3 sc in ch-3 sp, ch 10, sk 2 ch-3 sps, 3 sc in next ch-3 sp, ch 10, sk 1 ch-3 sp] rep around, join.

Rnd 17: Sl st to center sc, ch 5, [3 dc in

center of ch-10, ch 5, sc in center of 3 sc, ch 5] rep around, join.

Rnd 18: Sl st across 6 chs, [sc in each of next 3 dc, ch 10] rep around, join.

Rnd 19: Sl st in next sc, sc in center sc, ch 5, [3 dc in center of ch-10 lp, ch 5, sc in center of 3-sc group, ch 5] rep around, join.

Rnd 20: Sl st across 5 chs, [sc in each of next 3 dc, ch 10] rep around, join.

Rnd 21: Rep Rnd 19.

Rnd 22: Rep Rnd 20.

Rnd 23: Sl st to ch-10, [6 dc in ch-10 sp, ch 5, 11 sc in next ch-10 lp, ch 5] rep around, join.

Rnd 24: Ch 5, *[dc, ch 1, dc] in first dc, [ch 1, dc in each of next dc] 5 times, ch 1, dc in same dc, ch 5, sk 1 sc, sc in each of next 9 sc, ch 5, rep from * around, join.

Rnd 25: Ch 5, *[dc, ch 1, dc] in first dc, [ch 1, dc in next dc] rep across dc group with dc, ch 1, dc in last dc, ch 5, sk 1 sc, sc in each sc across to within last sc, sk last sc, ch 5, rep from * around, join.

Rnds 26 & 27: Rep Rnd 25.

Rnd 28: Ch 5, sc in first dc, ch 5, sl st in first ch to form a picot, ch 2, [sc in next dc, ch 5, picot, ch 2] rep across dc sts, ch 5, sc in center sc of sc group, ch 5, rep from * around, join, fasten off.

—Designed by Priscilla Graham

Your House of Happiness

Take what God gives, O heart of mine,
And build your house of happiness.
Perchance some have been given more;
But many have been given less.

The treasure lying at your feet,
Whose value you but faintly guess,
Another builder, looking on,
Would barter heaven to possess.

Have you found work that you can do?
Is there a heart that loves you best?
Is there a spot somewhere called home
Where, spent and worn, your soul may rest?

A friendly tree? A book? A song?
A dog that loves your hand's caress?
A store of health to meet life's needs?
Oh, build your house of happiness!

Trust not tomorrow's dawn to bring
The dreamed-of joy for which you wait;
You have enough of pleasant things
To house your soul in goodly state;

Tomorrow Time's relentless stream
May bear what now you have away;
Take what God gives, O heart, and build
Your house of happiness today!

—B. Y. Williams

Sunburst Surprise

Continued from Page 145

each of next 3 dc, dc in ch, dc in each of next 3 dc, dec over next 2 dc, ch 7, dc in ch-10, ch 7, rep from * around, join.

Rnd 14: Ch 3, *dec over first 2 dc, dc in each of next 5 dc, dec over next 2 dc, ch 8, 3 dc in next dc, ch 8, rep from * around, join.

Rnd 15: Ch 3, dec over first 2 dc, *dc in each of next 3 dc, dec over next 2 dc, ch 9, 2 dc in first dc, dc in next dc, 2 dc in next dc, ch 9, dec over 2 dc, rep from * around, join.

Rnd 16: Ch 3, *dec dc in next dc, dec, ch 10, 2 dc in next dc, dc in each of next 3 dc, 2 dc in next dc, ch 10, rep from * around, join.

Rnd 17: Ch 3, *dec over remaining 3 dc, ch 12, 2 dc in next dc, dc in each of next 5 dc, 2 dc in next dc, ch 12, rep from * around, join.

Rnd 18: Ch 3, *ch 12, 2 dc in next dc, dc in each of next 7 dc, 2 dc in next dc, ch 12, dc in dc, rep from * around, join in 3rd ch of beg ch-3.

Rnd 19: Ch 3, 2 dc in joining ch, *ch 10, 2 dc in next dc, dc in each of next 9 dc, 2 dc in next dc, ch 10, 3 dc in dc, rep from * around, join.

Rnd 20: Ch 3, dc in joining ch, dc in next dc, 2 dc in next dc, *ch 8, 2 dc in next dc, dc in each of next 11 dc, 2 dc in next dc, ch 8, 2 dc in next dc, dc in next dc, 2 dc in next dc, rep from * around, ending ch 8, join.

Rnd 21: Ch 3, dc in joining ch, dc in each of next 3 dc, 2 dc in next dc, *ch 6, 2 dc in next dc, dc in each of next 13 dc, 2 dc in next dc, ch 6, 2 dc in next dc, dc in each of next 3 dc, 2 dc in next dc, rep from * around, ending ch 6, join.

Edging

Rnd 1: Ch 3, dc in joining ch, *dc in each of next 5 dc, 2 dc in next dc, 5 dc over ch-6, 2 dc in next dc, dc in each of next 15 dc, 2 dc in next dc, rep from * around, join.

Rnd 2: *Ch 6, sk 1 ch, sl st, sc, hdc, dc, tr, sk 3 sts on doily, except for last point on which you skip 4 sts, sl st into next st, rep from * around, join, fasten off.

—Designed by Alice Heim

General Instructions

———⚜———

*Whether you are a beginner or seasoned crocheter, a doily
from this book will call out for you to pick up your hook and thread
and get busy crocheting.*

*The patterns included in this heirloom collection can be adapted to any
decor and taste, from antique to eclectic. Every doily is sure to be one you'll
enjoy displaying or giving as a special gift.*

*Following are instructions and diagrams that will assist you in
mastering the variety of stitches and techniques used in this book. You'll
also find interesting suggestions for displaying your beautiful work for all
to view and appreciate.*

*Enjoy expressing your love of crochet as you make these
lovely doilies stitch by stitch.*

General Instructions

Please review the following information before working the projects in this book. Important details about the abbreviations and symbols used and finishing instructions are included.

Thread

The doilies included in this book are worked in either size 10, 20 or 30 crochet cotton. Size 10 crochet cotton is the thickest of the three and will work up most quickly. Working with size 30 crochet cotton will give you a delicate look achieved because of the fine size. Although working with size 30 crochet cotton may take longer for some, most will agree that the beautiful effect it produces is well worth the effort. Crochet cotton is usually packaged in skeins or balls ranging from 150 yards to 450 yards. If you are working with an unusual color, be sure to purchase a little more thread than is called for to ensure you will have an adequate amount to complete the doily.

If desired, you may use a different size cotton than the one called for. However, you will need to change hook sizes and check your gauge in order to achieve the same size given. If you do not change hook sizes, realize that a doily worked with size 10 cotton with a size 7 steel crochet hook will be larger than the same pattern worked with size 30 cotton and a size 7 steel crochet hook.

Hooks

Crochet hooks are sized for different weights of yarn and thread. For thread crochet, you will use a *steel* crochet hook. Steel crochet hooks range from size 00 to 14. The higher the number of hook, the smaller your stitches will be. For example, a size 1 steel crochet hook will give you much larger stitches than a size 9 steel crochet hook. Keep in mind that the sizes given with the doilies' instructions were obtained by working with the size thread and hook given in the materials list. If you work with a smaller hook, depending on your gauge, your doily size will be smaller; if you work with a larger hook, your finished doily size will be larger.

Gauge

Gauge is determined by the tightness or looseness of your stitches, and affects the finished size of your project. If you are concerned about the finished size of the doily matching the size given, take time to crochet a small section of the doily and then check your gauge. For example, if the gauge called for is 10 dc = 1 inch, and your gauge is 12 dc to the inch, you should switch to a larger hook. On the other hand, if your gauge is only 8 dc to the inch, you should switch to a smaller hook.

If the gauge given in the pattern is for an entire motif, work one motif and then check your gauge.

Understanding Symbols

As you work through a pattern, you'll quickly notice several symbols in the instructions. These symbols are used to clarify the pattern for you: brackets [], curlicue brackets {}, asterisks: *.

Brackets [] are used to set off a group of instructions worked a number of times. For example, "[ch 3, sc in ch-3 sp] 7 times" means to repeat the instructions inside the [] seven times. Brackets also set off a group of stitches to be worked in one stitch, space or loop. For example, the brackets in this set of instructions, "Sk 3 sc, [3 dc, ch 1, 3 dc] in next st" indicate that after skipping 3 sc, you will work 3 dc, ch 1 and 3 more dc all in the next stitch.

Occasionally, a set of instructions inside a set of brackets needs to be repeated too. In this case, the text within the brackets to be repeated will be set off with **curlicue brackets {}**. For example, "[Ch 9, yo twice, insert hook in 7th ch from hook and pull up a loop, sk next dc, yo, insert hook in next dc and pull up a loop, {yo and draw through 2 lps on hook} 5 times, ch 3] 8 times." In this case, in each of the eight repeats of the instructions included in brackets, you will work the section included in curlicue brackets five times.

Asterisks * are also used when a group of instructions is repeated. They may either be used alone or with brackets. For example, "*Sc in each of the next 5 sc, 2 sc in next sc, rep from * around, join with a sl st in beg sc" simply means you will repeat the instructions from the first * around the entire round.

Stitch Abbreviations

The following stitch abbreviations are used throughout this book.

beg	begin(ning)
bl(s)	block(s)
bpdc	back post dc
ch(s)	chains(s)
cl(s)	cluster(s)
CC	contrasting color
dc	double crochet
dec	decrease
dtr	double treble crochet
fpdc	front post dc
hdc	half-double crochet
inc	increase
lp(s)	loop(s)
MC	main color
p	picot
rem	remain(ing)
rep	repeat
RS	right side facing you
sc	single crochet
sk	skip
sl st	slip stitch
sp(s)	space(s)
st(s)	stitch(es)
tog	together
tr	treble crochet
trtr	triple treble crochet
WS	wrong side facing you
yo	yarn over

"*Sk 3 sc, [3 dc, ch 1, 3 dc] in next st, rep from * around" is an example of asterisks working with brackets. In this set of instructions, you will repeat the instructions from the asterisk around, working the instructions inside the brackets together.

Blocking & Starching

Blocking and starching are done to a completed doily to give it a more finished look. Blocking will smooth out the doily and starching will help the doily to hold its smoothed-out shape.

Before blocking your doily, be sure all your ends are neatly woven into your work. To avoid having to weave in many loose ends after your doily is complete, weave ends in as your work progresses.

Nearly all doilies require light blocking and starching. Spray starch is available at grocery and household stores. Before starching, cover working surface with plastic wrap. To starch, lightly spray starch on doily. Press with an iron on medium heat, working from the inside rounds of doily and pressing out toward outer rounds. Allow to cool.

For heavier starching, purchase liquid starch. Following manufacturer's instructions, place doily in a sealable plastic bag with starch mixture. Work starch through doily. Remove doily and squeeze out excess. Using rustproof pins, pin doily to a piece of cardboard, placing pins in picots and stitches that you wish to accentuate. Allow to dry completely before removing pins.

Your Finished Doily

Every crocheter enjoys a sense of satisfaction when a friend or family member compliments her or him on a beautiful doily or tablecloth in her or his home. If you plan to place your doily on a table in your home, the following suggestions will allow you to enjoy your work for many years. To remove dust that accumulates weekly, simply shake out the doily once a week. Occasionally washing the doily by hand with a gentle soap will keep your work looking fresh and new. After washing, be sure to lightly starch and block your doily again.

Another lovely way to display a doily is to have it framed on the wall. Before framing, you will need to starch the doily heavily. Block the doily with pins on a piece of cardboard as explained above. For framing, select a mat to suit your decor. All professional framers will have a lovely selection of mats from which to choose. Finally, select a frame to your liking. You will also need to have the doily covered with glass or Plexiglas™ and sprayed with an adhesive to stick to the backing. A professional framer experienced in framing needlework will provide you with the best services to achieve the look you want.

To keep tablecloths looking their heirloom best, store them neatly folded and in a sealed plastic bag in a dry place. ❖

Stitch Guide

BASIC STITCHES

Front Loop (a)
Back Loop (b)

Chain (ch)
Yo, draw lp through hook.

Slip Stitch
Insert hook in beg ch, yo, draw lp through.

Single Crochet (sc)
Insert hook in st (a), yo, draw lp through (b), yo, draw through both lps on hook (c).

Half-Double Crochet (hdc)
Yo, insert hook in st (a), draw lp through (b), yo, draw through all 3 lps on hook (c).

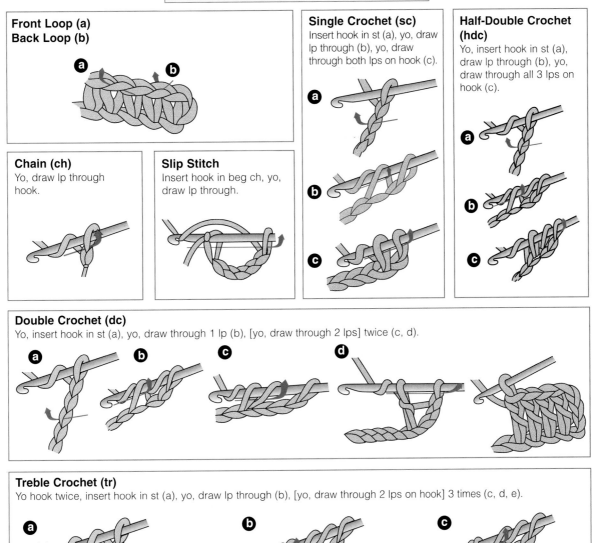

Double Crochet (dc)
Yo, insert hook in st (a), yo, draw through 1 lp (b), [yo, draw through 2 lps] twice (c, d).

Treble Crochet (tr)
Yo hook twice, insert hook in st (a), yo, draw lp through (b), [yo, draw through 2 lps on hook] 3 times (c, d, e).

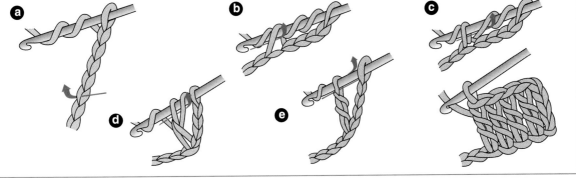

Double Treble Crochet (dtr)

Yo hook 3 times, insert hook in st (a), yo, draw lp through (b), [yo, draw through 2 lps on hook] 4 times (c, d, e).

Front Post/Back Post

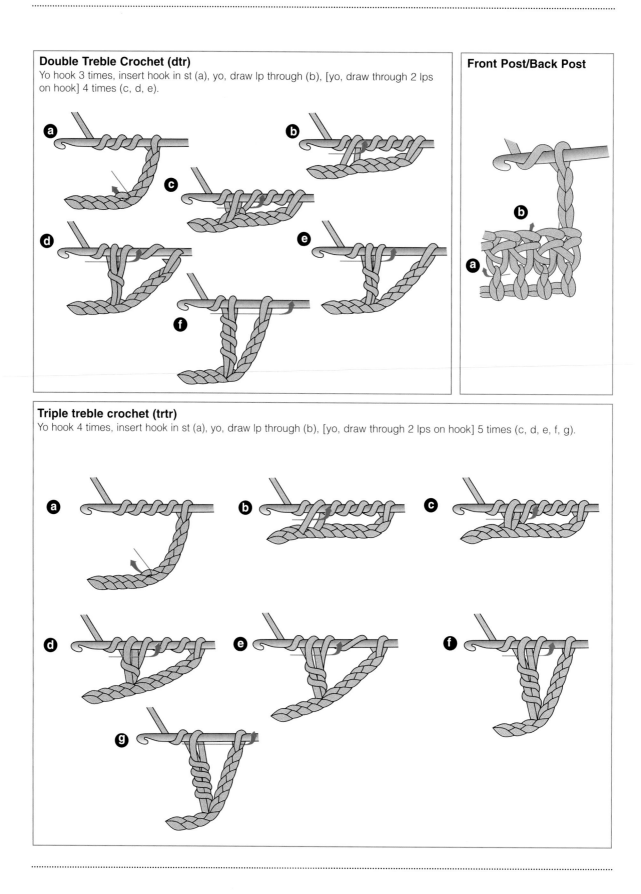

Triple treble crochet (trtr)

Yo hook 4 times, insert hook in st (a), yo, draw lp through (b), [yo, draw through 2 lps on hook] 5 times (c, d, e, f, g).

SPECIAL STITCHES

Reverse Single Crochet (reverse sc)

Working from left to right, insert hook in next st to the right (a), yo, draw through st, complete as for sc (b).

Chain color change (ch color change)

Yo with new color, draw through last lp on hook.

Double Crochet Color Change (dc color change)

Drop first color, yo with new color, draw through last 2 lps of st.

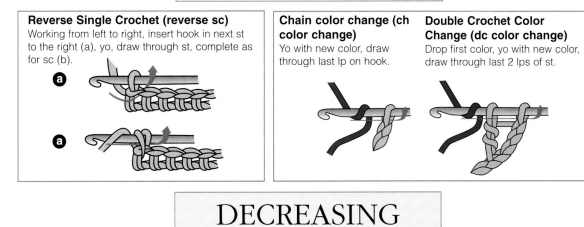

DECREASING

Single Crochet Decrease

Dec 1 sc over next 2 sc as follows: Draw up a lp in each of next 2 sts, yo, draw through all 3 lps on hook.

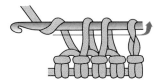

Half Double Crochet Decrease

Dec 1 hdc over next 2 hdc as follows: [Yo, insert hook in next st, yo, draw lp through] twice, yo, draw through all 5 lps on hook.

Double Crochet Decrease

Dec 1 dc over next 2 dc as follows: *Yo, insert hook in next st (a), yo, draw lp through (b), yo, draw through 2 lps on hook (c), rep from * once (d, e, f), yo, draw through all 3 lps on hook (g).

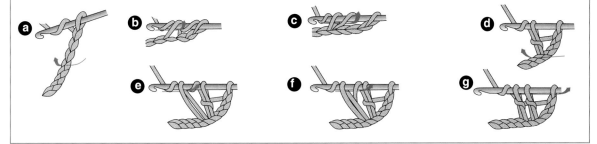

Index

Notes